Choosing Ethical Excellence

by Alan V. Funk

PUBLISHING CO.

©2006 by Alan V. Funk. All rights reserved
Printed in the United States of America

Library of Congress Control Number: 2006900700
ISBN 0-9747031-1-7

To contact the author via e-mail:
avf@chooseexcellence.com

For more information please write:
Promontory Publishing Co,
1204 E. South Temple Street
Salt Lake City, UT 84102

Table of Contents

Ethical Issues

Part 1

Introduction

" If it be a sin to covet honor, I am the most offending soul alive."[1] – *King Henry V*

Goodness makes good sense. I know this from experience. Having spent more than thirty years as a fraud investigator, including nearly five years as a special agent for the FBI, repeatedly witnessing the devastation that follows when people get caught breaking the rules, I can state with authority that making the effort to live a professional and personal life marked by honor and integrity is more than worth it. This is true, of course, not merely because unethical people risk being caught and ruined. Ethical excellence, the practice of consistently making the right ethical choices, has great rewards of its own, including increasing enjoyment in relationships and enhancing the overall quality of a person's life.

Agreement about what "goodness" means, or at least about what constitutes ethical behavior, is by no means universal in modern society. In the realm of business, where most of my investigations have taken me, there is even disagreement about whether a discussion of ethics is relevant at all. I believe, however, that such a discussion is not only relevant but urgent. Civilizations are built and preserved on the ability of people to trust one another and to work together for the common good. Without ethical underpinnings, relationships disintegrate, the strong can prey upon the weak, and the resulting disorder, even chaos, can ruin a life, a family, a business, a society.

Over the years, as I have identified and documented the existence of dishonesty and deception in private and public life, I have tried to understand why people choose behaviors that get them into trouble. At the same time, I have looked at my own values, considering how I would have reacted in circumstances such as those that led to the disgraces I was witnessing. In the process, I have come to certain conclusions about how people ought to behave in regards to one another. In my view, truly ethical behavior is not merely conformity to perceived conventional standards, not merely doing the minimum that is expected. Rather, people who are committed to ethical excellence, as I believe we all should be, will act according to unchanging principles and laws, not merely for what is in it for themselves, but also for the welfare of others.

This is easily enough said. It is not so easily done.

One of my sons graduated from college and began his career in consumer finance. After only a few weeks on his first job, he telephoned me: "Dad, I'm bothered by what I'm being asked to do at work. This morning one of the guys told me to put yesterday's date on a contract that wasn't signed until today. My boss is also asking *me* to witness signatures on official documents and to use *his* notary log to document those signatures when he's not present. That can't be right, and I'm sick about what he is asking me to do. I've challenged him face to face, and I'm afraid that if I keep complaining and refusing to do what he is asking me to do that I'll loose my job. Frankly, I'm not sure I even want this job. What should I do?"

My son was facing his first real ethical dilemma in the workplace - confronting a situation where his personal values were inconsistent with the practices established in this office prior to his arrival. All his life he had observed and read about my experiences investigating persons and businesses suspected of fraud. Yet, he did not expect when he entered the business world that he would be exposed so soon to pressures to do what he felt to be wrong.

As I framed a thoughtful response to my son's dilemma, I reviewed the conclusions about unethical behavior that had come to me over a long career of intimately dealing with the issues. Among the most significant of those conclusions is that avoiding unethical behavior requires a constant personal assessment of the pressures, opportunities, and rationalizations that accompany such behavior.

Like tens of thousands of young people before him have done, my son is entering the world of enterprise, learning that this world is exciting and dynamic, affecting the lives of nearly everyone on the planet, whether they produce, market, account for, consult with, or consume. In this complex world, making decisions about appropriate behavior can be particularly difficult. Such decisions naturally will be influenced by what is reasonable under current conventional standards. Often, acceptable business behavior is defined not by ethical considerations (what is *right*) but by practical or pragmatic considerations (what *works*, what brings the greatest perceived advantage). Suggesting that the ethical standard is preferable because it is "higher" than the strictly pragmatic can be seen as naïve, even foolish.

Being absolutely honest in a business transaction, or in a negotiation where bluffing and puffing are common practice, can indeed affect the outcome of the interaction. "This is my final offer." "This is the last one we have in stock." "This property was recently appraised at $350,000." People who are focused on the outcome of a transaction may find such statements acceptable, even if the statements are false. They may say, "That is just the way business is, and everyone knows it." Countering such attitudes and preventing them in one's self can be a persistent challenge for anyone, young or old, facing pressures to succeed in the business world.

My interest here is not to expose or disclose any specific misbehaviors but to alert others to what is regularly occurring in the workplace today and to help young people see a need to prepare for the challenges that they will undoubtedly face in their careers. Too often the process of learning how to act in the workplace takes the form of "on-the-job training." When that is the case, employees are more inclined to go along with the behaviors others around them exhibit, accepting those behaviors as "just part of the job." Activities such as pilfering, for example, could be perceived as part of an unofficial compensation package. Duty to an employer could justify a loosening of personal ethical standards. Loyalty to a boss could obscure an understanding that the obligation for loyalty is limited to requirements that are consistent with the legal and ethical objectives of the company.

In spite of pressures to compromise, however, workplace habits associated with ethical behavior can be changed for the better. The more important changes are those that affect a person's inclinations to make the right choices. While business entities can alter opportunities and incentives to encourage those changes, no amount of organizational controls can completely eliminate unethical behavior. It is important to believe that it is possible to survive and excel in the workplace while living a higher standard than what may be observed in others. My own search for answers to questions about how individuals should conduct themselves in their dealings with others has led me to conclude that there are choices that, if properly and consistently made, will bring enjoyment in ethical relationships.

In my view, the objective of ethical behavior should not be mere compliance with minimum ethical standards. Rather, the person who is committed to excellence is inclined to exceed those standards, not for the sake of what is in it for himself, but rather because he has developed a disposition to be better. Developing such a disposition requires conscious thinking about ethical behavior and an effort to learn ways to develop personal ethical standards and to avoid departures from those standards. This includes obtaining an understanding of rationalizations that lead to unethical behavior. It includes encouraging others to be more effective in being "impartial spectators of their own character and conduct"[2] and in taking time to prepare to follow through with ethical resolutions.

Choosing Ethical Excellence

Individuals can choose excellence in any number of areas of their lives. Some choose to be excellent in their careers. Some choose to be excellent in their marriages and their family life. Some choose to be excellent in issues related to their health and fitness. For most people, mere compliance with basic minimal standards in life's endeavors is not particularly fulfilling. It is excellence, reaching beyond what is "required" in any aspect of life, reaching for a higher standard, that brings true satisfaction. A choice for ethical excellence is like any other decision to reach beyond the commonplace. My identification of *Ethical Choices* is an attempt to provide some advice regarding how to rise above the minimum standard of ethical behavior.

In my view, excellent ethical behavior is empowering, not inhibiting. But affecting change in a mature person's ethical behavior is not easy. It often requires a serious interest in making a change and an understanding of how the change process works. Since I desire to promote change in the way people view ethical behavior, I have endeavored in these pages to convincingly describe helpful psychological and philosophical theories, so that others will be affected in a positive way. Ethical excellence requires concentration, commitment, and effort, but it leads to the kind of self-assurance that can contribute to a greater enthusiasm for work and to the peace of mind that is a gift to those who live a life of integrity. Naturally then, it is my expectation that proper consideration of the ideas discussed here will have a positive influence on workplace behavior.

My Personal Ethical Philosophy

Ethical behavior, consciously or unconsciously, is dictated by one's personal ethical philosophy - the assumptions, beliefs, and attitudes that govern the choices one makes in daily life. A number of such philosophies have been fully articulated by moral philosophers. I will examine some of these later in the book, and references to many of them may be found in the bibliography.

For now, I can distinguish between my own preference and a very common, scientifically based approach. The scientific approach suggests that in evaluating what constitutes ethical behavior it is inappropriate to conclude that one moral philosophy is more correct than another and that, except for the most obviously offensive acts, particular behavior may be ethically or morally correct or incorrect, depending on the particular philosophy to which one subscribes.

My own preference, on the other hand, is for a philosophy that accepts the existence of absolute principles and laws that are applicable to everyone. Such a philosophy emphasizes that our ethical choices should take heed of the welfare of others and recognizes that exceptions to absolute ethical principles are rare. In asserting that ethical choices should be made according to such criteria, I place myself in the company of countless men and women in modern times and throughout the ages who have pondered the issues and come to similar conclusions.

My task here was not to set forth a mere code of ethics. Codes of ethics may be found in a variety of professional and business organizations. Such codes, however, have their limitations. No persons exposed to significant interactions in a business environment are going to find all the answers to their moral dilemmas in a code. All persons need to be prepared to exercise moral judgment based on the ethical philosophy they have internalized. To maintain ethical moorings in a complex world, it is helpful to think carefully in advance, to prepare to make choices based upon a personal sense of propriety.

To assist in accomplishing this task, I have identified a series of fundamental decisions that anyone interested in ethical excellence can make. Such decisions, made early and attended to consistently, can provide a secure framework for a life of ethical excellence. I call these decisions *Ethical Choices*. None of the choices can be considered original thinking on my part. I have identified them after extensive reading of books, professional journals, and periodicals related to ethical behavior; thus they represent what I believe to be a consensus of wise thinkers.

Following is a brief introduction to the *Ethical Choices* I will discuss in this book.

Ethical Choices

1. Choose to be competent and diligent.

Education and experience allow people to become competent in their workplace activities. The body of knowledge associated with any work is constantly changing, so ethical people recognize the need to continue to learn those things that enable them to perform in an excellent way. Competent people recognize that their actions can affect the performance of others and can contribute to the success of their organization. Therefore, they encourage competent behavior by assisting in attracting others into their work who are similarly motivated, by assisting in their development, by setting an example of competence, and by rewarding competent behaviors. These persons recognize their limitations and undertake only those assignments that their education and experience have made them competent to perform.

Diligence implies performing in a prompt, careful, and thorough way. It further implies complying with technical and ethical standards and satisfying obligations owed to employers and to other stakeholders in an organization. Persons who are diligent are loyal to the worthy objectives of the organization.

2. Choose to establish a legacy of truth.

A high sense of integrity motivates ethical persons to be honest in the performance of their responsibilities. Standards of integrity are subject to interpretation. The person who has an interest in establishing a legacy of truth considers both the form and the spirit of the standards. Standards of truth are applicable to all phases of work. Representations of qualifications and accomplishments must be complete without leaving potentially inaccurate impressions. Errors and inadequacies should be disclosed.

In the business world, organizations sometimes engage in activities that are unethical. These activities can be carefully crafted to mirror the characteristics of legitimacy when, in fact, they are quite the opposite. Those who are interested in engaging in ethical activities need to be careful in choosing the organizations with which they wish to associate.

3. Choose to be other-centered.

Ethically excellent people are not motivated solely by self-interest. Ethical persons recognize that their individual success is dependent in great part on the existence of an extensive and reliable community of others who similarly trust in the integrity of the community. Ethical persons are involved in assisting others to achieve their worthy goals, and they avoid personal gain obtained from the disadvantage of others.

People who are members of professional organizations should be committed to advancing the worthy objectives of their organizations. This includes assisting in raising the standards of excellence within their professions through training and performance monitoring.

4. Choose to comply with the demands of economic justice.

Economic justice implies more than just engaging in transactions where the buyer and the seller are treated fairly. It refers to three principles: equivalence, distributive justice, and contributive justice. Equivalence involves exchanges of goods and services at fair prices. Distributive justice relates to associations between persons of authority with persons who work under their control. Persons with greater authority are expected to be fair in the distribution of both the benefits and the burdens to those under their control. Contributive justice relates to responsibilities to the groups with whom individuals and companies associate. Individuals derive benefits from their associations with these groups and, therefore, owe a duty to them to support their activities and not to act in such a way as to discredit the other members.

5. Choose to be thorough and critical in decision-making.

Determining how much effort should be expended in arriving at correct choices can be a significant challenge. Too often, people find themselves involved in a dangerous condition known as "groupthink," where members of a group fail to independently question the correctness of decisions. The interest in showing respect for the thinking of others, being "team players," and rationalizing decisions can override the perceived need to carefully consider the correctness of important decisions.

Difficult decisions often require careful deliberation. I have identified a process that should be helpful in making those decisions. This process involves investigation, analysis, and discussion with others. Writing down facts, potential solutions, and support for conclusions is an important part of the process.

6. Choose to follow through with ethical resolutions.

Complying with personal ethical standards requires a significant commitment. Unethical behavior occurs when three factors are present: a pressure, an opportunity, and a rationalization. People can avoid unethical behavior by controlling or eliminating any of these elements, which may involve recognizing personal weak moments, associating with respectable people, and realizing the unique pitfalls of a particular profession.

All people face challenges when they witness behavior that is inconsistent with the objectives of the organization and, in some cases, inconsistent with the law. There are times when it is appropriate to "blow the whistle" on the wrongdoer.

7. Choose to be an impartial spectator of personal character and conduct.

Adam Smith, in *The Theory of Moral Sentiments*, identified his "whole man" as a man with a social conscience. One of the most difficult challenges in achieving the objective of being a whole man or a person of integrity lies in being able to step out of one's own skin and to see one's self as one really is. The goal must be praiseworthy behavior. The ability to live a life of integrity will be dependent in large part on whether a person has a clear and disciplined conscience and an abundance of goodness.

When people have to make critical decisions, they are often faced with conflicts of interest, which are situations where their personal interests are inconsistent with the responsibilities of their position. The challenge is to recognize these conflicts and to deal with them in a way that is acceptable.

Codes of Ethics and Ethical Choices

In the 1980s, a time when written codes of ethics were not as common as they are now, representatives from Johnson & Johnson conducted an interesting study. They identified fifteen companies which had written codes of ethics. They then measured the appreciation, over a period of thirty years, of a hypothetical stock investment of $2,000 per company, a total investment of $30,000 in these fifteen companies, and compared it with the investment of an identical amount in the stocks of the Dow Jones Industrial Average. After thirty years, the value of the $30,000 investment in the fifteen companies with written codes of professional ethics was over $1 million. The Dow Jones composite investment over the same period was worth only $134,000.[5]

Not surprisingly, most major companies and professions now have written codes of conduct that deal with such matters as conflicts of interest, relationships with suppliers and customers, fair employment practices, and reporting violations of ethical standards. These statements of ethical policy can be useful tools in establishing the conventional standards and procedures of the entity or profession. All of these entities recognize the value of these codes, and companies certainly will benefit from compliance with their codes. The important question is whether they are a part of the entity's real culture.

I did not use any particular corporate or professional codes of ethics to identify the decisions comprising my *Ethical Choices*. However, these codes proved to be a valuable source for affirming the completeness and accuracy of these *Choices*. While all codes focused their articles, principles, and canons on the unique requirements of their professions and companies, they often addressed the same unique choices I have identified principally from other sources of ethical thought. Throughout the chapters describing the *Ethical Choices*, I have included excerpts from the codes of ethics of various companies and professions as a reinforcement of my descriptions. Readers who are interested in focusing on their line of work may find certain of these references particularly interesting.

Discussions of the *Ethical Choices* comprise **Part 2** of this book. Before embarking upon these detailed discussions, I will offer, by way of orientation, a real-world example of the kind of ethical thinking and behavior I most admire and contrast it with a widely held point of view I find less worthy. I will then present a brief analysis of ethical theory as it has been explored by moral philosophers ancient and modern. To conclude **Part 1**, I will spend some time examining the treacherous path that leads from unethical choices to fraudulent behavior.

The ancient poet Dante beautifully articulated, in the opening lines of *Inferno*, this common human perplexity.

> Midway upon the journey of our life,
> I found myself within a forest dark,
> For the straightforward pathway had been lost.

Those who find themselves in the "dark forest" of unethical behavior could profit from considering the choices outlined here as a means of returning to the light. But perhaps even more importantly, those who are just setting out upon the path of adult human endeavor could profit from learning to make such choices a part of their ordinary way of thinking, their routine way of acting, at home and at work, in private life and in society.

It is important to learn these things early, and to be alert to their application at all times. The temptations to stray from the straightforward path are great, and the voices counseling something other than ethical excellence come from surprising sources that can seem, at first, to make sense. Prior to my entering Marine boot camp some of my associates advised, "Don't be first, don't be last, blend into the disappearing middle, and don't volunteer for anything." It took me about a week to discover that "blending into the middle" was against my nature. Over the course of a lifetime I have discovered again and again that mere compliance with minimal standards in most areas of life is not particularly fulfilling.

And so, I present the *Ethical Choices* described in this book as guides that enable people not only to avoid the moral quandaries that are found in the workplace and in other aspects of their lives, but also to motivate them to aim higher than ethical mediocrity, and ultimately to lead to their choosing the fulfilling practices of ethical excellence.

Notes

1   William Shakespeare, *Henry V, Act IV, Scene III*.

2   Adam Smith, *The Theory of Moral Sentiments* (Indianapolis: Liberty Fund, 1984), 114.

3   Surendra Arjoon, "Virtue Theory as a Dynamic Theory of Business," *Journal of Business Ethics* 28 (2000): 160.

Ethical Excellence in the World of Business

" **If American businessmen are right in the way most of them now live, then all the wise men of the ages, all the prophets and the saints were fools. If the saints were not fools, the businessmen must be.**"[1]

– Louis Finkelstein

"Don't worry about it. It's just business." We have all heard this kind of talk. And perhaps most of us know that the person speaking is trying to excuse bad behavior. Unfortunately, the excuse usually works. In fact, it is commonplace in the modern world for people to believe, or at least to feel fine about professing to believe, that the wisdom of the ages no longer applies, and that what is good is not what is right, but what you can get away with.

In striking contrast to such ethical cynicism is Aaron Feuerstein. For thirty years Feuerstein was President and CEO of Malden Mills, the multi-generational, family-owned business he joined in 1947 following his graduation from New York City's Yeshiva University. A devoutly religious Jew, Feuerstein ran his company according to the other-centered principles of his faith, the "driving force in his life" being the ancient precepts taught him by his father: "When everything is moral chaos, try your hardest to be a 'mensch,' or man of highest principles."[2]

Malden Mills has been a New England-based fabric mill for more than 140 years. The primary business emphasis of Aaron Feuerstein has always been the creation of a quality product with highly skilled, well-paid employees who utilize superior technology. Maintaining a satisfied and loyal workforce has been a hallmark of Malden Mills. As Bob Fawcett said of his boss, "We're treated fairly. I mean, you'd better produce; he doesn't give it away. But he takes care of people. But more than just in salary. If you're hurting, you're in trouble, you got a place to go."[3] Another employee, Jackie Hosty, added, "I actually had two brain surgeries, but because of him I was able to get the doctors I needed."[4]

Over the years Malden Mills has maintained a research and development department that has attempted to develop unique products to keep the business successful. On occasion, their product manufacturing emphasis has been brilliant and successful, and, on occasion, it has not. In the early 1980s, manufacturing emphasis was in artificial furs, but then the demand for artificial furs collapsed. Over the next few years, the company was saved when its R&D department developed a new synthetic fabric that was lightweight, weather resistant, and wool-like and that was sold under the brand names Polartec and Polarfleece. These fabrics have since been used in both outerwear and upholstery manufacturing.

Aaron Feuerstein believed he could find the skilled textile workers that would allow him to compete effectively in Lawrence, Massachusetts. And so that is where he located the plant in 1956. In the mid-1990s when textile workers were paid an average of $9.50 per hour, the Malden Mills employees were paid $12.50. Market pressures had years before forced many of the textile manufacturers to flee the northeastern United States to the South where they found cheaper labor and laws "friendlier" to business. Malden Mills elected to stay in New England. Evidence of a satisfied workforce is found in its employee retention and productivity statistics. In the 1990s, Malden Mills' employee retention rate was in excess of 95 percent. From 1982 to 1995, the workforce of Malden Mills doubled, while its revenues more than tripled.

As with most mature businesses, Malden Mills has faced times when conditions have forced a downsizing of their workforce. Feuerstein believes there is such a need as "legitimate downsizing." He says, "Legitimate downsizing as the result of technological advances or as a result of good industrial engineering? Absolutely. I'm in favor of it. And we do it here all day long. . . . We try to do it in such a way as to minimize human suffering, but the downsizing must be done." He continues, "The trick is to keep growing fast enough to give new jobs to the people technology displaces, to weed out unnecessary jobs without crushing the spirit of the work force."[5] Feuerstein is critical of others who implement "downsizing that is a result of the CEO searching for cheaper labor elsewhere."[6]

In 1980, as a result of the disastrous move into the fake fur business, Malden Mills was forced to declare bankruptcy and had to lay off workers. After the huge success of the Polartec product, Feuerstein was able to rehire every employee he had laid off during the bankruptcy. By 1995, Malden Mills was generating $400 million per year in revenues and $20 million in pre-tax profits.

In December 1995, Feuerstein's commitment to his "highest principles" was put to a test. As he was celebrating his seventieth birthday, he was notified that his factory was burning to the ground. Three of its major manufacturing facilities were completely destroyed. It was reported to be the largest fire in Massachusetts in 100 years and one of the largest in New England history. Although no one was killed in the fire, the whole town was devastated, since Malden Mills was one of Lawrence, Massachusetts' largest employers.

As Feuerstein stood watching the fire destroy his business, he thought "How can I possibly recreate it? I was proud of the family business and I wanted to keep that alive, and I wanted that to survive. But I also felt the responsibility for all my employees, to take care of them, to give them jobs."[7]

What were Feuerstein's options at that moment? First, he could accept a $300 million insurance settlement and retire. But Feuerstein later reasoned, "And what would I do with it? Eat more? Buy another suit? Retire and die?"[8] Furthermore, he reasoned, had he taken the insurance money it would have hurt his employees and the whole town of Lawrence. "What kind of an ethic is it that a CEO is prepared to hurt 3,000 people who are his employees [and] an entire city of many more thousands . . . in order for him to have a short-term gain? It's unthinkable."[9] Feuerstein's second option was to use the insurance money to rebuild in the South or overseas where the labor was cheaper. His third option was to rebuild in Lawrence, and that is what he chose to do.

But what would become of the 1,400 workers who would be left jobless while Malden Mills rebuilt? He would pay them as if they were still productively employed at the factory, and that included both wages and health-care benefits. His reasoning, he reported, is consistent with his understanding of the Torah. "You are not permitted to oppress the working man, because he's poor and he's needy, amongst your brethren and amongst the non-Jew in your community."[10] His decision would prove costly - $25 million, in fact. Years later, Feuerstein commented, "I think it was a wise business decision, but that isn't why I did it. I did it because it was the right thing to do."[11]

Obviously, word of Feuerstein's generosity got out. He was praised in the major newspapers, magazines, and on television. He was a guest of the President of the United States at the State of the Union address. He was praised by columnists and religious leaders. He received thousands of letters from throughout the country. He received twelve honorary degrees, many of them doctorate degrees from major universities.

Feuerstein's reaction to the attention was predictable. "Fifty years ago, it would have been considered very natural for a CEO, if his plant burned down, to rebuild it and to worry about his people and . . . his community and city. Today, business leaders have lost their allegiance to their workers and communities and remain loyal only to the shareholder - all in the name of short-term profits." Feuerstein continues, "There's some kind of crazy belief that if you discard the responsibility to your country, to your city, to your community, to your workers, and think only of the immediate profit, that somehow not only your company will prosper but the entire economy will prosper as a result, and I think it's dead wrong."[12]

More significant, however, was the reaction of his 3,200 employees. Those left with positions at Malden Mills worked at a "frenetic pace" to bring the operation back. Within three months, two of the three divisions were up and running at nearly full capacity. Over 2,500 of the employees were back to work. The extra effort of the employees at one portion of the facilities not destroyed by the fire resulted in a production of twice the usual yardage per week. Improvements in the quality of the finished product were also realized. Instead of producing six to seven percent off-quality output, the factory improved to just two percent off-quality.

Feuerstein has his critics. Some of the criticism goes to Feuerstein's motives, asserting that his generosity was motivated not by pure altruism or high-minded principle but by an expected return from his employees of increased production and quality. These same critics point out that there were financial advantages to having the insurance companies pay for the rebuilding of the facilities on the same site rather than accepting an insurance settlement amount that would be based on a depreciated value of the lost real and personal property. Others criticize Feuerstein's decision as simply foolish. One business magazine writer used particularly harsh language in describing this point of view. "Much of this celebrity is based on the misleading premise that this 70-year-old acted selflessly, against his own interests, which is another way of saying that he acted the way a saint might act: irrationally." He adds, "In fact, it seems pretty clear that some people call Feuerstein a saint because they don't quite have the courage to call him a fool."[13]

To such accusers, Feuerstein might counter that "not all who increase their wealth are wise," and that "in a situation where there is no righteous person," one should "try to be a righteous person," regardless of what others may think about one's motives.[14]

As the owner of his business, Feuerstein had more freedom to act as he did as long as he was using his own money. For Feuerstein, his freedom to act independently of other stakeholders became more restricted subsequent to the fire. Feuerstein received the $300 million insurance proceeds, borrowed another $100 million, and built a more "environmentally friendly and worker friendly" facility. This decision, not unlike the fake-fur decision and the fire, proved to be the next major crisis for Feuerstein. With the continued financial pressures on the United States textile industry and with heavy debt, Malden Mills was again forced to file a Chapter 11 bankruptcy.

Now critics spoke out with particular sharpness. One utilitarian analyst suggested that it was not Feuerstein but Jack Welch, former CEO of General Electric and much maligned as the "epitome of the greedy capitalist"[15] who should be praised. In the moral universe of this critic, "the creation of wealth and the innovation and technological advancement that comes with it - even when motivated by greed - is the clearest and most effective way to better the human condition."[16] And in the end, says this critic, it was Jack Welch, not Aaron Feuerstein, whose practices produced the most good for the most people.

> Aaron Feuerstein's good heart nearly cost the
> economy the 3,000 jobs Malden Mills employs.
> Sure, it's swell that 3,000 families could continue
> to pay rent, to buy clothes, and to put gas in
> the car. But was it really the most honorable of
> Feuerstein's options, as his enthusiasts insist? . . .
> Aaron Feuerstein gave away $25 million of wealth.

His charity did little more than help a few thousand people maintain their present standard of living. It didn't create new jobs. It did nothing to better the condition of anyone other than Aaron Feuerstein and the people who got his money.

Jack Welch - driven by profit - laid off 100,000 people 20 years ago. But he's since built enough wealth for GE to employ several times that many people - including, now, the 3,000 who work for Malden Mills. . . . Not only has Jack Welch done more than Aaron Feuerstein for humanity, he's actually done more for the employees of Malden Mills.[17]

As one university professor and "expert on corporate responsibility" suggested, "it may have been that the desire to take principled action somehow blinded [Feuerstein] to thinking long term."[18]

But for Aaron Feuerstein and those who share his moral views, human beings "are charged with acting not for the moment but rather for the larger goal,"[19] and Feuerstein's critics have it "exactly wrong, of course. Long term was precisely what he was thinking."[20]

The story of Malden Mills points out many issues that are relevant to a study of business ethics. Among the more important ones are social responsibility, ethical excellence, monetary generosity, and creditor responsibility. It is profitable for us to consider questions regarding each of these issues.

1. Did the business entity, Malden Mills, have a social responsibility to the community of Lawrence, Massachusetts? Was Feuerstein, therefore, obligated to consider the interests of the community in deciding whether to accept the insurance proceeds and retire, whether to continue to pay his employees as he rebuilt, or whether to relocate to the South?

2. Because some of Aaron Feuerstein's generous actions related to the rebuilding of the plant in Lawrence and the continuing payment of wages for displaced workers had predictable positive consequences, should Feuerstein have been honored for being ethically excellent?

3. When Malden Mills added $100 million to its debt burden, was Aaron Feuerstein still free to continue in his generous ways?

4. If the cause of the Chapter 11 bankruptcy can be tied to the construction of expensive, environmentally sound and worker friendly facilities, and the "predictable consequences" were an overly burdensome debt structure, was Aaron Feuerstein acting irresponsibly in regard to his creditors?

Social Responsibility in the World of Business

One of the important debates among the experts of business ethics relates to whether businesses have social responsibilities beyond generating the greatest level of profits for the owners of the business. Aaron Feuerstein demonstrated a significant interest in social issues beyond the earning of a profit. He paid wages and insurance benefits to displaced workers that he had no obligation to pay. When downsizing became necessary, he was generous in assisting the displaced workers. His decision to rebuild in Lawrence, Massachusetts, was based, in part, on his concern for the well-being of the residents of the local community. When he rebuilt his facility, he built one that was more environmentally and worker friendly.

Those who espouse the idea that business has an extensive social responsibility identify the stakeholders (i.e., those who have a legitimate interest in the activities of the business) more broadly than just its owners and lenders. The broader view of stakeholders would include the workers, managers, customers, suppliers, unions, competitors, and the local community. This point of view recognizes that society exists for the benefit of and betterment of its members, and when people participate as members of society they should, if they have any sense of the contributions that these other stakeholders make to their betterment, recognize that they have obligations to them. Otherwise, they are mere freeloaders.

An opposing point of view suggests that the notion that businesses have a social responsibility to contribute to the "common good" is nothing more than socialism.[21] Economist Milton Freedman, for example, argues that those who run corporations are agents of the owners (the shareholders) and as such have a direct responsibility to carry out the wishes of the owners. Generally, that means making as large a profit as possible while conforming to the laws and ethical customs of society. Those same corporate officers are entitled to do all the good they wish for their communities, as long as they are using their own funds and their own time. When they do so, they are "acting as principals" rather than agents of their employment.[22]

There are multiple considerations in deciding which of these alternative views is correct. First, it is important to consider that there is a hierarchy of responsibilities in society. People make choices that can restrict their ability to carry out what they perceive to be other important obligations to society. When I choose, for example, to borrow money to purchase a house, I make direct promises that I am obligated to keep at the expense of other choices, even though the other financial choices are important to the betterment of society. If I expect to live a life of integrity, I should be willing to disclose to my lender whatever my intentions are with respect to meeting my special obligations to him. Likewise, as an employee, I make special and direct promises of loyalty to my employer. The hierarchy of responsibilities in an employment setting is first to the law and then to my employer. My causes, special interests, and sympathies may have to take a lower priority to the interests of the law and of my employer.

In the case of Malden Mills, when the plant burned down, $100 million was borrowed from outside entities. Those who contracted with the outside financial institutions no doubt made certain commitments associated with the careful and responsible use of the $100 million in the reconstruction and in the operation of the business. They were expected to ensure that Malden Mills would have the ability to repay the financial obligations when they became due. Behavior inconsistent with keeping these promises is not justified. To suggest otherwise is to suggest that making promises and keeping commitments should not be taken seriously.

A second consideration is deciding who the legitimate

stakeholders of a business are and how they are properly dealt with, which is a subjective matter. Suppose, for example, that for the sake of having a strong employer such as Malden Mills in town, property tax concessions are extended and all of the local residents are obliged to bear some additional burden. One could effectively argue that the local community is a stakeholder and that the business has at least an implied obligation to the community that sacrificed for its benefit. Another could oppose this notion and argue that the business fulfills whatever obligation it may have to the community by doing its best to be successful, thereby providing the jobs for which the community hoped.

A third consideration is that in a free economy, except for obligations for the payment of taxes imposed by governments, individuals and owners of entities should be free to utilize their resources in whatever legal fashion they choose. Society does not require more from business entities. Ethically excellent behavior, however, would contemplate a broad recognition of who the stakeholders are and a willingness to contribute something back, according to capacity, to the society that contributed to the betterment of the business entity.

Applicability of Personal Ethics to the Workplace

Another interesting debate exists regarding whether all aspects of personal ethical behavior are applicable in the workplace.

Consider James, for example. James considers himself an ethical person. He believes that he is no better and no worse than the next guy, as far as living an ethical life. On Saturday morning he gets together with his friends and plays basketball.

James's strength on the basketball court is his one-on-one ability. He can fake his opponent out with the best of them and then drive to the basket to score. On Sunday he regularly attends his local church and worships with his family. He accepts as true the teachings that are taught there and believes it is appropriate that he live by them. On Monday he goes to work where he sells automobiles. It is James's understanding that there are certain rules and practices utilized in his business in order to be successful in making sales. One rule is that salesmen have to be aggressive. That means that salesmen have to bluff and occasionally bluff hard. James rationalizes that these are standard practices in the business and are consistent with those followed by others within his company, that they have an excellent product that the customer will enjoy, that nothing he does is illegal, and that it is important that he get ahead in life in order to support his family. James feels justified in faking and bluffing on Monday through Friday at work and on Saturday on the basketball court. After all, business is sort of a game with special rules, isn't it?

In 1968 an article appeared in the *Harvard Business Review* that challenged the notion that personal ethics are applicable in a business environment. Even today this article is a staple for ethics classes where, in the name of intellectual challenge, it presents a rather persuasive argument that business has "the impersonal character of a game" and, therefore, its own "special ethics." The article's author, Albert Z. Carr, reasoned that since the government has set the rules of the business game and "as long as a company does not transgress the rules of the game set by law, it has the legal right to shape its strategy without reference to anything but its profits." He concludes that only strategy and not ethics should affect the way a business person treats customers, employees, and others.[23]

Mr. Carr's premise is that business strategy is not unlike the game of poker where bluffing is a recognized part of the game. In business, as in the game of poker, unless people are willing to occasionally avoid telling the "whole truth," they will be denied certain successes. Mr. Carr reasons that in "office lives [businessmen] cease to be private citizens; they become game players who must be guided by a somewhat different set of ethical standards."[24]

Mr. Carr recognizes that a "reputation for integrity, honesty, and decency" will improve chances for success, but he warns that there are some situations where the choice is bluff "within the legal rules of the game" or lose. His advice in such cases? Businessmen should "bluff - and bluff hard."[25] Mr. Carr further warns, "If an executive allows himself to be torn between a decision based on business considerations and one based on his private ethical code, he exposes himself to a grave psychological strain."[26]

Since the publication of Mr. Carr's article, there have been significant efforts within the business ethics academic community to challenge Mr. Carr's premise. Unfortunately, Mr. Carr's descriptions reflect the reality of much of the workplace, and little of what the academicians suggest is going to alter the departures from ethical behavior found in business dealings.

Mr. Carr, of course, is not alone in the position that ethics in business are irrelevant. The late Peter Drucker, who is well-known for his writings on management practice, has written that business ethics not only are not needed,[27] they are hostile to business,[28] and irrelevant.[29] He has further concluded that "the ethical position . . . becomes pure sentimentalism - the position of those who believe that evil can be abolished and harmony established by good intentions."[30]

A Brief Response to Mr. Carr's Notion of Business Bluffing

Those arguing against applications of ethics to business are too often forced to use the argument that "that is just the way business is done" and consider the disadvantages to self. As I mentioned in the opening of this chapter, most of us, making an honest reflection, can realize that this line of argument is more of an excuse than a justification. Granted, business has as its primary purposes the production of goods and services for profit and the means for an effective distribution of goods and services. However, human beings, truly precious assets, are affected by the exchange of those goods and services, and that fact makes fair and moral behavior associated with those activities appropriate.

Finding bluffing and other deceptive business practices to be unacceptable has strong philosophical justification. One of the most profound and influential moral thinkers of modern civilization, Immanuel Kant, insisted that it was an affront to human reason for one person to treat another as a means to an end, rather than as an end in himself. When one person bluffs another, the intent is to use the weakness or ignorance of one party to improve the outcome for the other. For Kant, this would be an unnatural (unreasonable), and therefore immoral behavior.

It is true that in some situations the bargaining process involves advocating, and an essentially equal exchange. When both parties are fully informed of the methodology and both parties are adequately prepared to be involved in this form of price setting, bluffing may be an acceptable practice. But if this methodology is not understood and deemed acceptable by both parties, the bluffing by one person, to gain unfair advantage over another, is not ethically acceptable.

Some exchange transactions are so unique and generally non-recurring that the buyer is often ignorant of the value of the product and the nature of the bargaining process. Buying a wedding ring would be one such example. Generally the seller has superior knowledge of the value of the stone(s) and the setting and the techniques of selling. The buyer, under the influence of the romantic feelings of the moment and ignorant of the real value of the product, could be persuaded to make a financially foolish decision. In that situation the real value of the ring could be significantly less than its purchase price. An ethical seller would want to assess the understanding of the buyer and to determine what information to disclose to the buyer in order to make the transaction fair. Further, the sales representative should also consider that the buyer is looking to the sales representative not only as an advocate of his product but also as a consultant whom he trusts to help him determine what he needs.[51]

This highlights a significant problem with the approach that allows bluffing. Consider the extreme example. Suppose the buyer is impaired in some serious way. He has a permanent mental deficiency, he is under the influence of alcohol or drugs, or, in the case of the ring buyer, he may be under the influence of a romantic feeling. Would it be appropriate for the seller to take advantage of that person's deficiency in the bargaining process? At what level of impairment, then, are businessmen ethically permitted to take advantage through bluffing of the other person's deficiency? Whether the other person in the transaction has a permanent impairment or a temporary one, or whether superior skill and knowledge allows him to create an impairment in the dealing, taking unfair advantage in such a situation is offensive to the ethical person.

The argument against inappropriate forms of business bluffing also becomes apparent when considering the purposes of the market system. The market system is designed to provide buyers and sellers an opportunity to exchange goods and services for something of value. Any activity that tends to place a party to these transactions at a disadvantage is a distortion of the purpose of the free-market system. In the marketplace willing buyers meet with willing sellers, both hoping to be able to come away with value. The marketplace should be a place where superior product and superior efficiencies are rewarded, rather than a place where superior deception occurs.

There are some business transactions where a trusting relationship between the buyer and seller is so critical that bluffing is never acceptable. The relationships between lawyer and client and doctor and patient are examples. The superior knowledge and skill of the lawyer and the doctor and the need for clients and patients to place their absolute trust in the other are so significant that bluffing and deception in these relationships would be unconscionable. That is the reason why these and other professions develop codes of professional ethics that are, in part, intended to protect those who rely on the services of the professionals.[32] Consider these references.

> A physician shall uphold the standards of professionalism, be honest in all professional interactions ...[33]

> Engineers . . . shall not distort or alter the facts.[34]

> [Accountants] . . . perform all professional
> responsibilities with the highest sense of integrity.
> Integrity requires a member to be . . . honest
> and candid within the constraints of client
> confidentiality.[35]

If people accept the idea that for a business transaction to be fair it must be based on arm's-length dealings, then they should be offended by the idea that business bluffing is acceptable. Arm's-length dealings imply not only willing sellers and willing buyers, but also a sufficient understanding of the facts relevant to the dealing. Any form of deception would be inconsistent with an arm's-length deal.

Albert Carr and others who attempt to justify business bluffing compare business activities to a game of chance, such as poker, where the rules are unique to the activity. Carr argues that everyone with any business sophistication should understand the unique nature of the rules of business and, therefore, should be prepared to act consistently with what the rules allow. But enterprise should not be turned into a game of chance. Engaging in enterprise involves the distribution of precious goods and services. Unless we can imagine a society in which gambling is considered an appropriate means for distributing wealth, we must agree that any form of enterprise based upon deception is wrong.

Businessmen justify a system of capitalism based in large part on the notion that actions motivated by self-interest result in the promotion of the interests of society and in the creation of jobs, products, services, and investments. However, self-serving efforts to deceive, to coerce, and, thereby, to artificially create inequality are inconsistent with the proper objectives of a capitalistic system and, therefore, are wrong.

The reality is that the business world is full of people who think and act contrary to the ideals I advocate. It is improper to suggest that those who choose not to engage in these deceptive practices as they participate in their business transactions should accept the role of victim of the deceptive behavior. Rather, businessmen should be willing to do the homework necessary to become familiar with the people and the environment they will encounter, prior to engaging in business transactions.

Let me offer an example of what I mean. Several years ago I purchased a house in California. It was a tract house where comparable houses were being regularly sold by the owner-developer. The sales office provided a brochure that quoted a price. Before I made my counter offer, I visited the County Recorder's Office to determine the lowest price the developer had accepted in recent months for the same model in a similarly situated location. That became the basis for my offer. The sales person acted surprised when the owner accepted my offer. I had done my homework. I felt no need to bluff and, in the end, I felt confident that my purchase price was fair. I had treated the seller with honesty and respect.

Weighing the Alternatives
-Does it pay to be ethical?

There is a natural tendency to try to weigh the advantages and disadvantages of acting ethically. While it is tempting to suggest that people ought to emphasize the advantages, I have no intention of doing this. Why? Because the gains that are derived from ethical actions should have nothing to do with motivations to be ethical. If my *Ethical Choices* are merely calculated efforts to derive advantage, then I am focused on something other than ethical excellence. Emphasizing ethics for the pay and the profits is a self-serving activity. Acting ethically is the right choice to make because goodness demands such a choice.

"Honesty isn't any policy at all; it's a state of mind or it isn't honesty." – *Eugene L'Hote*

Code of Ethics Guidance
Regarding Ethical Excellence

From the corporate world:

ExxonMobil Corporation: "The methods we employ to attain results are as important as the results themselves. The Corporation's directors, officers, and employees are expected to observe the highest standards of integrity in the conduct of the Corporation's business."

ExxonMobil Corporation: "The policy of ExxonMobil Corporation is to comply with all governmental laws, rules, and regulations applicable to its business. The Corporation's Ethics policy does not stop there. Even where the law is permissive, the Corporation chooses the course of highest integrity."

ExxonMobil Corporation: "The Corporation's directors and officers support, and expect the Corporation's employees to support, any employee who passes up an opportunity or advantage that would sacrifice ethical standards."

Wal-Mart: "When Sam Walton founded Wal-Mart Stores, Inc., he established the 'Three Basic Beliefs' to which we remain firmly committed. Respect for the Individual. Service to our Customers. Strive for Excellence. The Three Basic Beliefs go hand in hand with the integrity and ethical conduct that is the foundation of our business."

Wal-Mart: "Wal-Mart is committed to the highest ethical standards in the conduct of our business."

Wal-Mart: "Where there is a conflict between ethics and business objectives, ethics must always come first."

Home Depot: "Doing the right thing while performing your job may not always seem the easiest choice or the fastest way, however at the Home Depot, it is always the only choice and the only way."

Home Depot: "Our Values are our beliefs, principles and standards that do not change over time."

Home Depot: "We promise to maintain a safe and healthy workplace for all of our Associates and to treat everyone with respect and dignity. We will be fair and foster a highly ethical environment worthy of our Associates' loyalty and pride. We are committed to a workplace that encourages new ideas, high quality work, career opportunities, a balance between work and family and an entrepreneurial spirit."

Home Depot: "The Home Depot believes that all people should be treated with dignity."

Citigroup Inc.: "We aspire to be known as a company with the highest standards of ethical conduct – working to earn client trust, day in and day out."

Citigroup Inc.: "Citigroup expects all of its representatives to act in accordance with the highest standards of personal and professional integrity in all aspects of their activities and to comply with all applicable laws, regulations and company policies. We must never compromise that integrity, either for personal benefit or for Citigroup's purported benefit."

Microsoft: "Excellence in everything we do."

AT&T: "One of our values is that all employees are held to the highest standards of integrity."

Boeing: "The highest standards of ethical business conduct are required of Boeing employees in the performance of their company responsibilities."

The Kroger Co.: "The Kroger Co. has established a strong reputation for integrity in our business. To maintain and enhance that reputation, it is important for each of us to adhere to the highest moral, ethical and legal standards."

Berkshire Hathaway Inc.: "The Company . . . will continue to uphold the highest levels of business ethics and personal integrity in all types of transactions and interactions."

Notes

1   Louis Finkelstein, "The Businessman's Moral Failure," *Fortune* (September 1958): 116.

2   Shelly Donald Coolidge, "'Corporate Decency' Prevails at Malden Mills," *The Christian Science Monitor*, March 28, 1996:1, 9.

3   CBS News,"The Mensch of Malden Mills," http://www.CBSNews.com, July 6, 2003.

4   CBS News,"The Mensch of Malden Mills."

5   Thomas Teal, "Not a Fool, Not a Saint," *Fortune*, November 11, 1996: 201-202.

6   Coolidge, "Corporate Decency," 9.

7   CBS News, "The Mensch of Malden Mills."

8   CBS News, "The Mensch of Malden Mills."

9   Coolidge, "Corporate Decency," 1.

10 CBS News, "The Mensch of Malden Mills."

11 CBS News, "The Mensch of Malden Mills."

12 Coolidge, "Corporate Decency," 9.

13 Teal, "Not a Fool, Not a Saint," 201.

14 Rabi Avi Shafran, "Aaron Feuerstein, Bankrupt and Wealthy," http://www.aish.com, September 30, 2005.

15 Radley Balko, "Invisible Hand v. Visible Handout," http://www.techcentralstation.com, September 16, 2002.

16 Balko, "Invisible Hand v. Visible Handout."

17 Balko, "Invisible Hand v. Visible Handout."

18 Balko, "Invisible Hand v. Visible Handout."

19 Shafran, "Aaron Feuerstein, Bankrupt and Wealthy."

20 Shafran, "Aaron Feuerstein, Bankrupt and Wealthy."

21 Milton Friedman, "The Social Responsibility of Business is to Increase its Profits," *The New York Times Magazine*, September 13, 1970: 33.

22 Friedman, "The Social Responsibility of Business," 33.

23 Albert Z. Carr, "Is Business Bluffing Ethical?" *Harvard Business Review*, January-February 1968, 143-153.

24 Carr, "Is Business Bluffing Ethical?" 145.

25 Carr, "Is Business Bluffing Ethical?" 153.

26 Carr, "Is Business Bluffing Ethical?" 149.

27 Peter F. Drucker, *Management: Tasks Responsibilities, Practices* (New York: Harper & Row Publishers, 1973), as quoted in Michael Schwartz, "Peter Drucker and the Denial of Business Ethics" *Journal of Business Ethics* 17 (1998): 1686.

28 Peter F. Drucker, *The Changing World of the Executive* (Time Books, 1982), as quoted in Michael Schwartz, "Peter Drucker and the Denial of Business Ethics" *Journal of Business Ethics* 17 (1998): 1686.

29 Peter F. Drucker, *Post-Capitalist Society* (New York: HarperBusiness, 1993), as quoted in Michael Schwartz, "Peter Drucker and the Denial of Business Ethics," *Journal of Business Ethics* 17 (1998): 1686.

30 Peter F. Drucker, "The Unfashionable Kierkegaard," *The New Markets and Other Essays* (1971).

31 David M. Holley, "Information Disclosure in Sales," *Journal of Business Ethics* 17 (1998): 637.

32 Holley, "Information Disclosure in Sales," 633-634.

33 American Medical Association, "Principles of Medical Ethics," June 2001, Principle # II, http://www.3-media.com/ama.html.

34 National Society of Professional Engineers, "NSPE Code of Ethics for Engineers," Item III.a, http://www.nspe.org/ethics/eh1-coed.asp.

35 American Institute of Certified Public Accountants, "Code of Professional Conduct," Section III.

Text Box Footnotes

Eugene L'Hote, "Honesty isn't any ..." Ted Goodman, ed., *The Forbes Book of Business Quotations* (New York: Black Dog & Leventhal Publishers, Inc., 1997), 410.

Ethical Excellence: What, Why, and How

Why did he do that? What was she thinking? I have frequently asked myself such questions as I have investigated fraud and deception in public and business life. These questions are to some degree rhetorical, merely expressing my disbelief or dismay at the predicaments people get into when they deviate from the path of ethical behavior. But on another level these are real questions, and I have spent a good many years, much thought, and considerable research trying to find answers to them. In the process, I have discovered that if we can come to a general understanding of some basic and widely accepted notions about human motivation and human behavior, we can begin to be alert to the meaning of the ethical choices of others, while at the same time increasing our own capacity to make consistently correct choices.

Such general explanations have both philosophical and psychological dimensions. This means that to evaluate ethical choices we have to understand both *what* constitutes ethical behavior and *why* and *how* people respond to ethical issues.

Moral Philosophy, or What Constitutes Ethical Behavior

How does a person decide that what he is doing is "right"? What makes someone stop, deciding that her choice to behave in a certain way would be "wrong"? The challenge to define what is ethically or morally right is complicated by the fact that different people have different perceptions regarding what constitutes acceptable behavior. Essentially, however, ethical belief systems may be categorized as based on philosophies that are either *relative* or *ideal*.[2]

In deciding what is ethically right, a *relativist* looks at the circumstances and probable consequences of a choice, while an *idealist* is focused to a greater extent on particular notions (*ideas*) of "truth and right, goodness and beauty, as standards and directive forces."[3]

A person high on the relativism scale (see Figure 1), someone we might call a strong relativist, would consider cultural factors and personal feelings in making ethical choices. A person at the low end of the relativism scale, on the other hand, believes that whether an action is morally right depends on whether it complies with rules, norms, and laws. This person will rely on the belief that his first duty is to obey the rules, expecting that the rules will yield the right results.

A person high on the idealism scale (see Figure 2), one we would call highly idealistic, is strongly motivated, by compelling notions of rightness and goodness, to look out for the welfare of others. On the opposite end of the idealism scale is the person who is motivated more strongly by a desire to satisfy personal needs.

Figure 1	Figure 2
Situation & Consequence Based	Other-Centered

High — Relativism — **Low**

High — Idealism — **Low**

Rules, Norms, Laws Based   Self-Centered

Most people would find the extreme positions on either of these scales to be fairly undesirable. At one extreme of the relativism scale we might find a person who is so rigidly tied to rules that he cannot consider the possibility that strict adherence to rules might not yield the best result, or that there might not be a rule for every possible situation. At the other extreme we might find a person who is so averse to finding any one point of view to be better than any other that he will accept no absolute rules about anything.

At the extremes of the idealism scale we might find a person who is completely self-centered, having no regard for the interests of others, or on the other end a person who becomes overwhelmed, even paralyzed by his concerns for the needs and opinions of others.

Except for generally rejecting these extremes, however, people differ widely in opinions about where it is good to be on the scales of relativism and idealism.

An enlightening exercise combines the relativism and idealism scales into quadrants that define four distinct kinds of moral philosophies (see Figure 3). These philosophies have been identified as *Situationist* (Quadrant I), *Absolutist* (Quadrant II), *Exceptionist* (Quadrant III), and *Subjectivist* (Quadrant IV).[4] Each philosophy possesses a unique combination of either high or low relativism and high or low idealism.

Figure 3

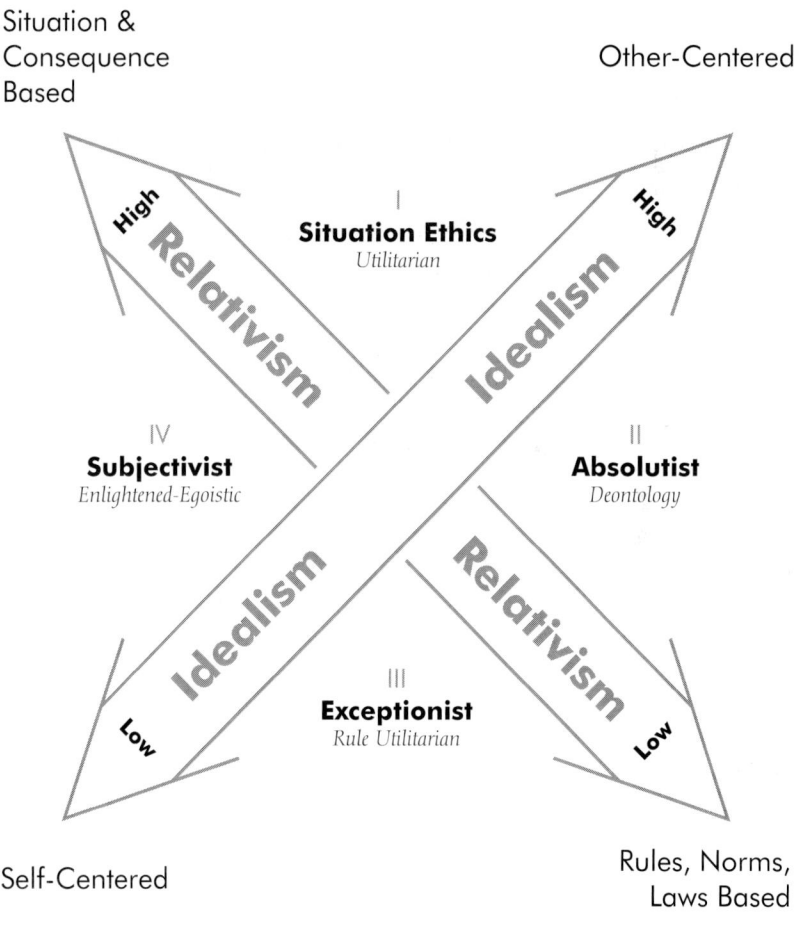

Situation &
Consequence
Based

Other-Centered

High

Relativism

I
Situation Ethics
Utilitarian

Idealism

High

IV
Subjectivist
Enlightened-Egoistic

II
Absolutist
Deontology

Idealism

Relativism

Low

III
Exceptionist
Rule Utilitarian

Low

Self-Centered

Rules, Norms,
Laws Based

The other-centered quadrants

Quadrants I and II represent moral philosophies that are other-centered and are, therefore, called *theories of obligation.*[5]

Quadrant I represents a moral philosophy that has as a dominant feature the determination of what is right and wrong based on an evaluation of the consequences of the act. The action that is right is the one that yields the most benefit and the least negative consequences to all affected people. *Utilitarianism* is the most common form of situationist moral philosophy.

" **The pursuit of the objects of private interest, in all common, little, and ordinary cases, ought to flow rather from a regard to the general rules which prescribe such conduct, than from any passion for the objects themselves.**" *– Adam Smith*

Much of the problem-solving thinking in today's business world is particularly focused on utilitarian ethics. Cost-benefit analysis and maximizing profits are utilitarian ways of arriving at solutions. Jeremy Bentham and John Stuart Mill were major proponents of utilitarianism.

A criticism of utilitarianism is that the determination of what constitutes the greatest good and the least harm is made by the person acting, and, therefore, tends to seem arbitrary to those affected by the action.[6] Another criticism is that the costs and benefits of any particular behavior or course of action can be difficult to determine.[7]

Quadrant II has as its dominant feature the determination of what is right and wrong based on an evaluation of rules and principles. In its most strict form, such a philosophy deems actions to be ethical when those actions conform to the moral rules, "regardless of the consequences of so doing."[8] This kind of moral philosophy, called *deontology* (from a Greek word meaning *obligation* or *necessity*), recognizes universal or absolute moral principles. The Judeo-Christian codes and traditions, and the thinking of the Greek Stoic philosophers are largely associated with a deontological approach to moral reasoning. The categorical formulations of the German philosopher Immanuel Kant are likewise deontological.[9]

Critics of a strict deontological approach note the impossibility of devising a rule for solving every possible human dilemma. This criticism has particular relevance in a society where change is rapid. Other criticisms focus on the harshness and inflexibility of absolute or categorical systems in the face of human realities. A strict deontologist might believe, for example, that truth-telling is a moral absolute, and therefore would not condone lying, even if it appeared to be necessary to save human life.

The self-centered quadrants

Quadrants III and IV represent moral philosophies that tend to be self-centered. Most people could find little justification for accepting a philosophy that is identified primarily with self-centeredness, so these quadrants might be viewed more in terms of allowing self-interest to dictate actions, as long as others are not purposely and arbitrarily hurt by the action.

The Quadrant III moral philosophy suggests that "conformity to moral rules is desirable,"[10] but that exceptions are often appropriate, and those exceptions tend to be self-benefiting, such as in a business setting with the need to maximize profits. This moral philosophy is sometimes referred to as *rule-utilitarianism*.

In Quadrant IV the tendency is to reject moral rules and to base the determination of the rightness of the situation on personal feelings. People adhering to such a "subjective" philosophy are highly focused on their own best interests. They act to promote their own self-interest as long as those actions do not unfairly or arbitrarily hurt others. They feel no obligation to strive to produce positive outcomes for other people.[11] This moral philosophy is sometimes referred to as *enlightened egotism*. A similar philosophy is *rational egoism*, preached by novelist-philosopher Ayn Rand and popularized in her novels *The Fountainhead* (1943) and *Atlas Shrugged* (1957). Rand's philosophy likewise rejects the moral significance of other-centered behavior ("altruism" in such a philosophy is not a virtue), but in emphasizing reason rather than personal feelings as the proper basis for moral action, Rand called her philosophy *Objectivism*. Former Federal Reserve Chairman Alan Greenspan was, early in his professional life, attracted to the ideas of Ayn Rand.

Setting aside Quadrants III and IV for the moment, I can illustrate the distinction between consequence-based (Quadrant I) and rule-based (Quadrant II) behavior with a personal example.

The t-shirt sale

When I was sixteen my summertime employment was in the men's clothing section of a local department store. Even though I was the junior person in this department, I was allowed to sell everything but suits to the customers of the store. The store sold quality merchandise, and I suspect I was one of their best teenaged customers since a substantial portion of my pay ($1.25

per hour in 1963) went to buying my own clothing. In my view, only one of our products was inferior to something that could be purchased elsewhere. Our t-shirts were not as thick as those sold by J.C. Penney, which happened to be a couple of doors down the street. I bought my t-shirts at J.C. Penney.

A woman came into the store to buy clothing for her son. I helped her with a few items, but then she told me she wanted to buy her son some t-shirts and specified that she wanted to be sure they were the kind that were popular at the local high schools. I knew that our t-shirts were not what she was looking for. What should I have done? Since I truly believed her son would not be satisfied with our t-shirts, should I have made the sale anyway?

The choice I faced can be used to illustrate two basic approaches to making ethical choices. Utilitarian reasoning might work like this: There are multiple interests in this t-shirt transaction. The son needs a good t-shirt. The customer is interested in buying something that will satisfy her son. She needs my advice to help her choose the right product. The store is interested in sales, but it is also interested in satisfied customers. Of course, neither she nor I can predict with *complete* accuracy that her son would be dissatisfied with the t-shirt I could sell her. However, I am confident, based on my personal observations of others, that if her son expects to be properly dressed, he needs the J.C. Penney t-shirt. If I send her to J.C. Penney, my employer will lose the sale of a package of t-shirts, but the department store might gain in its reputation with this customer. Notice that this reasoning is focused on the *consequences of the transaction* rather than on my duty as an employee of the store.

Deontological reasoning, on the other hand, would include duty as a primary consideration. Thinking this way, I might reason that my employer is the one who compensates me, and he has a reasonable expectation that I will be loyal to him. While there is no specific rule saying that "an employee will sell our merchandise and only our merchandise," neither is there any rule or department practice authorizing me to sell clothing for J.C. Penney. Because I am not authorized to do so, and in fact probably have a duty not to do so, I should not be directing a customer to a competitor. Of course, I can at the same time also reason as a deontologist to a different conclusion. If I consider that my duty of complete honesty to my fellow creatures, including the customers of the store where I work, is a "higher" duty than duty to my employer, I will send my customer to J.C. Penney.

We should briefly consider here a third moral system, one we will explore in greater detail at the end of this chapter, in the discussion of how and why people respond to moral issues. Like deontology and utilitarianism, this system of thought is "normative," that is, it says something about how things ought to be, instead of merely describing how things are. This philosophy is commonly called *virtue ethics*, because it focuses on personal virtues or positive character traits as the source of ethical behavior.

Approaching the t-shirt dilemma as a virtue ethicist I would be acting out of my personal inclinations, and the process might go something like this: I am a good person, and a good person is honest (J.C. Penney t-shirts are better, and I know it), forthright (when a customer makes a request, it is up to me to respond in a useful way), generous (even if it means losing a commission, I should regard the needs of my customer), and so on. Acting in accordance with the kind of person I am, or desire to be, I send my customer to J.C. Penney. Of course, a virtuous person is also dutiful and loyal, which could bring my employer back into the picture.

The t-shirt dilemma teaches us that a particular resolution of a moral quandary is not entirely dependent upon the method of moral reasoning employed. What else may come into play?

Ethical behavior has been the subject of extensive theorizing for thousands of years, and any attempt to summarize or simplify, or even to select one system for preferential consideration, risks doing injustice to the wealth of information that exists about a great many carefully-worked-out systems of thought. Nevertheless, to explain the moral underpinnings of the *Ethical Choices* I will be examining in **Part 2** of this book, it is useful to take a brief look at the framework or strategy for testing the moral rightness of actions developed by Immanuel Kant. No one has had a more significant impact upon deontological ethical theory than has Kant.

Kantian ethics

We can explain Kant's scheme for evaluating morality as a consideration of the imperatives that govern human action. An imperative declares an action, or inaction, to be *necessary*. An imperative may be *hypothetical*, stating what is necessary in a particular circumstance: "To get to the top in this job, I'm going to have to work ten hours a day and not worry about whose toes I have to step on." Or an imperative may be *categorical*, stating what is true for all people in all circumstances: "A person must never cheat in order to gain an advantage over others." A categorical statement such as this is a *maxim*, a statement of a fundamental principle. For Kant, if a maxim can be universalized, that is, made into a law that all must follow, it is moral. But if an imperative cannot be followed without "contradiction," or without harming the autonomy of others, it is not moral.

For Kant, the source of moral maxims was "nature" - not necessarily God or any Supreme Lawgiver, but Reason - the natural ability of the human mind to come to a logical, non-contradictory conclusion about how all human beings should behave. In other words, in Kant's view the human brain is hard-wired with *categories* that dictate moral imperatives. For Kant, a belief system based merely on *hypothetical* imperatives could never be moral because it would be too subjective, too open to changing interpretation, too likely to be irrational and contradictory. In the example above, for instance, I may work ten hours daily, step on toes and ruin all my personal relationships, and still never "get to the top." Someone else may get ahead of me by cheating, or by working harder, or by being nicer to people, or by marrying the boss's daughter. And even more importantly for Kant, if everyone behaved according to this hypothetical imperative, the process of job advancement in general could be ruthless and chaotic.

So, for Kant, morality could not be a matter of merely asserting taste or personal preference. Morality was deeply rational, absolute, and unchanging. In order to determine the rightness of particular actions against an absolute standard, valid for all human beings, Kant devised a test based on what he called the *categorical imperative*, which he expressed in three formulations, each focusing on a different aspect of the morality of human behavior. To simplify Kant's framework somewhat, an action would be considered ethical (1) if it is capable of being universally applied, (2) if it shows respect for other rational human beings, and (3) if it originates from a notion of respect for the autonomy of other human beings.[12] According to Kant, if the action fails to pass any one of the formulations, it is not moral.

Kant expressed the first formulation as follows: "Act only on that maxim by which you can at the same time will that it should become a universal law."[13] Under this "Formula of Universal Law," the expectation is that if something is right for me, it must be right for all other rational human beings. This formulation should not be mistaken for what we commonly call the Golden Rule. In the Kantian universe, the imperative "do unto others as you would have them do unto you" might be unreliable. I may be weak or full of self-loathing and therefore might be willing to accept abuse or the lies of others, and thereby justify abusing or lying to others. The categorical imperative demands that a maxim should be suitable for all, not just for the person acting in a given circumstance.

Suppose, for example, that I am considering lying to my intended employer about my background on my employment application. Kant would have me construct a general principle that defines what I intend to do. In this case, the general principle is that lying to my future employer is acceptable behavior. Then I would ask if it would be appropriate to make a general rule to allow all people to lie on their applications of employment (especially when it appears to be necessary to get the job). When I evaluate that situation, I must conclude that no matter how successfully I might rationalize my own decision to lie, to allow lying in this situation as a general rule would destroy the value and purpose of the employment application. Because the intended act is contradictory to the purpose of the application process, the action cannot be considered moral.

This process seems simple and obvious, but Kant's first formulation of the categorical imperative is the one most often ignored.[14] Many people are convinced that rationalizing in such a circumstance is true and useful reasoning. (Regardless of apparent inadequacies in my background, I deserve the job and know I would do it well. So my lie is actually the right thing, even the necessary thing to do in this situation, and I would fully expect anyone else to do the same thing in my position.) And few people are willing to accept that lying is never appropriate. Many people find no ethical problem, for instance, in "the little white lie," with telling people they look good when they do not, or with misrepresenting the exact truth in order to protect others from serious and undeserved harm or consequences. A strict Kantian, however, would always tell the truth, regardless of the consequences.

The second formulation of the categorical imperative reads, "Act so that you treat humanity, whether in your own person or in that of another, always as an end and never as a means only."[15] This formulation has been referred to as the "Formula of Humanity"[16] because it requires that people consider the dignity and worth of others affected by their actions. Complying with this formulation would require that, in all action, a person must treat others with respect and never think of another as a mere tool to be used to accomplish an end, such as meeting the financial goals of an organization. Under this formulation, deceiving and coercing are forbidden.[17]

The third formulation, the "Formula of Autonomy," or the "Formula of the End in Itself," requires that people respect the autonomy of their fellow creatures. For Kant, human beings are "autonomous" because they alone of all creatures on earth possess the capacity for rational choice. This gives to human beings "a moral status that Kant labeled 'dignity' and he built his entire moral theory around the idea that this status is to be respected and protected."[18] The third formulation of the categorical imperative implies that human beings must be free to choose the course of self-perfection without compulsion or coercion. In order to avoid using others as tools, all persons must exercise self-control in taking account of the moral status of others. Moral action will

" Moral behavior is far more common when utility conspires with duty, and the strongest moral codes are invariably those that are supported by considerations of both advantage and obligation."

– Henry Sidgwick

be motivated not by a desire to be rewarded by happiness or by an impulse to serve some utilitarian end. Rather, moral action arises from the independent reason of the moral person, identifying principles of justice that can apply universally to all people.

The Kantian ideal of the supremely rational moral agent, acting upon invariable principles regardless of personal need or situational variation might seem a strange creature to many in the modern world who may tend to treat questions about right and wrong as "relative to individual values and cultural diversity."[19] And, in fact, I should emphasize once again that regardless of the differences in the process of resolution, actual solutions to moral quandaries may be the same whether one uses a deontological or a utilitarian approach. It is likewise important to emphasize that, on occasion, in dealing with particularly challenging ethical quandaries, moral ("virtuous") people must be prepared to consider *both* the rules *and* the consequences of the action. In fact, consideration of others may lead such people to act outside either a utilitarian or a deontological profile. To such idealists, any "what's in it for me" behavior would be deemed to be unethical.

Most people, in fact, accept the notion that circumstances can require a departure from an accepted rule, that extreme emergency circumstances may justify a departure from law, as when a highway speed limit is disregarded while taking a seriously injured person to the hospital or when a Dutch householder lies to protect Jews hiding in the closet from being captured by Nazi soldiers. We may say, in fact, that a person who would not violate the law or even his own ordinary moral rules in such a circumstance is rigid, inflexible, or uncaring, even weak in character, or lacking in virtue. And now that we are making assertions such as these, we are in the realm of human psychology.

Psychological Theory, or Explaining Why and How People Respond to Ethical Issues

People have differing ways of confronting ethical issues, depending upon their moral belief systems, of course, but also depending upon their personal needs, intelligence, preparedness, ability to empathize with others, and general strength of character, which includes an ability to act independently of the pressures of outside influence. Such psychological factors, reflecting what we might call moral maturity, largely determine why and how people respond to ethical dilemmas.

We can make only the briefest exploration here of human psychology, but even a quick look at some widely accepted theories can move us forward in our understanding of how to make consistent ethical choices. We can first make some general statements about ethical decision-making as, undoubtedly, we have all observed it.

There are those who understand the correctness of a given situation and its related consequences, but, for the sake of personal benefit, choose an unethical solution without worrying about any justification. A business negotiator finding himself disadvantaged in a conflict may lie, skew the facts, engage in puffery, knowing that he is being dishonest and that dishonesty is generally wrong, but since "this is business," he has no qualms at all about doing whatever is necessary to gain the advantage in the negotiation.

At the opposite end of that spectrum, others with the same knowledge and understanding deliberately choose an ethical solution. A negotiator committed to the value of honesty and integrity in dealing with others, regardless of personal gain or loss, will avoid distorting the truth in an attempt to gain power or profit at the unfair expense of others.

Still others, through ignorance or inexperience, fail to recognize ethical issues when confronted with them and, consequently, fail to give special attention to their ethical choices. A beginning negotiator or new employee, caught off guard in a difficult situation, may simply say or do what comes to mind, making no conscious effort to deceive or harm, just trying to keep his head above water and not make a fool of himself. He may be sorry later, when he thinks about what he has done, but he may feel that he had no other choice.

Finally, there are those who recognize the existence of ethical challenges, but find solutions only by rationalization, and those solutions are generally according to the consequences that provide the most favorable personal benefits.[20] An employee may understand that, under pressure, or in confusion, he has done something wrong, something that violated his own principles or even his employer's code of conduct. He may worry about this at first, but since he got away with it, he may begin to construct in his mind a psychological reality in which what he has done is okay. Perhaps what he did (got away with) increased his esteem among his colleagues, or brought an advantage to the company and a raise in his future. Maybe, then, what he did was not so wrong after all.

What follows is a discussion of two psychological theories that attempt to explain why and how persons respond to ethical issues. The first focuses on stages of moral development. It reasons that moral behavioral differences are explained by the fact that people act consistently with their level of moral maturity. The second focuses on the internal and external forces that influence decisions about moral issues. An awareness of both theories allows for a better understanding of the thinking processes that affect ethical decisions.

Lawrence Kohlberg's moral development levels

The late Lawrence Kohlberg wrote extensively on the subject of moral awareness and human development.[21] He identified the differences in moral behavior on a scale marked by six stages of development falling into three major levels of moral maturity. Kohlberg's model is not perfect. Based solely on a study of males, it has been criticized for allowing an interpretation that some have seen as resulting in a certain kind of gender bias.[22] The model is useful, however, in helping us understand moral behavior in a typical work-related environment.

To explain Kohlberg's model, I have created the example of John, an insurance salesman. We will define "success" for John as including effective work performance, valued contribution to his employer, and personal satisfaction. While some jobs may not require moral development beyond the first stage (making small rocks out of large ones in a prison setting comes to mind), success in most work is enhanced as a person advances in the stages of moral development. This will be the case for Salesman John.

Pre-conventional level. At Kohlberg's level one, a person has learned to distinguish between good and bad and right and wrong based on the outcomes of the behavior exhibited. The motivation to do the good and the right comes from the desire for the expected consequences of the action - consequences that will benefit the person himself. The behaviors exhibited at this level are typical of children.

The pre-conventional level is broken down into Stages 1 and 2. At Stage 1 the person is focused totally on the physical consequences to himself. A child may learn to avoid throwing his food if he knows the consequence is to have an important toy taken away. The child eats his vegetables if he knows that is what is necessary to get dessert.[23]

> At Stage 1 level of moral maturity, John reports his
> sales and shows up for office meetings each week
> because, in order to keep his job, he is required to
> do so. Every sale contributes to his commission
> income. It matters little to him whether the policy
> he sells is in the best interests of the buyer; he
> is in it for the revenues the sale contributes to

him personally. He is not interested in bringing in
the expertise of others on difficult sales because
that would require him to share the commission
income with another. He is something of a gambler:
he would rather take his chances on the sale than
split the commission. He is more interested in
closing the sale than fully describing the limitations
of the policy. If the buyer should later express
dissatisfaction with certain aspects of the policy,
that's too bad; the paperwork is done, and it's too
late to make a change.

In Stage 2 the behaviors are still focused on the expected
outcomes, but elements of fairness and sharing enter into the
actions. However, the motivation to be fair and share originates
from pragmatic considerations. The child will share his toy
with another if he knows he can play with the toy belonging
to the other. The child will help his sister make her bed if he
knows his sister will reciprocate. Notice that at both of the
pre-conventional stages of moral development the person is
focused primarily on himself, viewing others as the source of
rewards and punishments.[24]

Maturing to Stage 2, Salesman John operates in
much the same fashion as he did before, except
that he has now discovered that cooperating with
others who have superior knowledge on certain
aspects of the insurance products can help him
close some of the difficult sales. He has to share
the commission on those sales with others, but
as long as those same agents bring him in on

sales where he has developed an expertise and
can contribute to their success, he is willing to do
business with them; it is only fair that they share.
John keeps track of commission income he has
given up to others and commission income he
has earned by contributing his expertise on the
sales of others. If the commission sharing ledger
gets out of balance with respect to any of John's
fellow insurance colleagues, John is less inclined to
continue cooperating with that colleague.

Conventional level. At the conventional level, attention is given
to family, community, and group expectations. The person sees
value in participating in behaviors that are consistent with
those of others based on his contribution to the social order.
Conformity and loyalty are important at this level. The person
who operates at this level may be inclined to believe that ethical
standards vary between his home and his work and that what is
ethical at work is whatever the boss says it is. Conventional level
workplace behavior is legal and consistent with the established
practices of the employer.

The conventional level is divided into Stages 3 and 4. In
Stage 3, the person is motivated by the satisfaction he receives
knowing he is conforming and pleasing when abiding by the
behaviors that are natural, typical, and appropriate. The person's
good intentions are significant to the evaluation of the behavior.
Being "nice" and "meaning well" are important.[25]

At Stage 3 John feels a sense of accomplishment
when his efforts contribute to the success of the
insurance company. After all, the stronger and

better-recognized the insurance company is, the more likely John will be successful in his efforts. John enjoys the recognition of being the top salesman of his office, not just for the rewards it gives him beyond his earned commissions, but that plaque on the wall is quite an honor. John observes the proven, successful sales techniques of others in the office and adopts them as his own. While his product may be inferior in some ways to others, effective sales technique requires that he avoid disclosure of those aspects to potential insurance clients.

Stage 4 is focused on rules, laws, and their contributions to social order. The person focuses on respect for authority, personal duty, and the "social order for its own sake."[26] At this stage the person will recognize that others around him may be conforming to behaviors that are common, but could be improper. The person operating at this level is inclined to obey the rules because he respects what they represent.[27]

When John operates in Stage 4 he pays attention not only to the local practices but also to the rules established by the national office and the governmental agencies that regulate his profession. He feels respect for his bosses and his profession. John attends seminars where he learns how to best serve his clients and his profession. He becomes active in his professional society, is familiar with its code of ethics, and does his best to comply with the provisions of that code.

Post-conventional, autonomous, or principled level. At the post-conventional level, the person is focused on "moral values and principles that have validity and application apart from the authority of the groups or persons holding these principles and apart from the person's own identification with these groups."[28] While his interest will be focused on the good and order of society, the actions of this person are motivated by the rightness of the action. At this level, loopholes are shunned because they are contrary to the spirit of the rule or law. Others are seen as ends rather than just as means to an end, a view Kant's second formulation of the categorical imperative suggests is appropriate.

Kohlberg refers to Stage 5 as the "social-contract legalistic orientation." Because behaviors in this stage are focused on individual rights and society's standards, there are evidences of utilitarian thinking in this stage. Consensus thinking is an important part of this stage since personal values and opinions of others are important in the process of determining what is right and good. The law is a point of emphasis, yet the possibility exists that the law may need to be changed for the sake of the benefit of the society or group.[29]

> In Stage 5 John begins to think and act based on principles that seem right at a more universal level. While he feels a sense of loyalty to his employer and his product, he sometimes recognizes that his company's product is not "all things to all people" and that the client may be better served with a product that John cannot sell. He is willing to sacrifice a commission for the sake of the good of his client. John recognizes that, on some

occasions, his contribution to the good of a sale is not significant, and he may need to back off on a demand for participation in a commission that the "rules" could allow. Answering the phone and referring a sale to another may not justify a shared commission.

In Stage 6 the person makes decisions that are based on an evaluation of his conscience and his ethical principles. The factors that contribute to the reasoning applied at this level of moral action are "logical comprehensiveness, universality, and consistency."[30] Kohlberg cites a biblical comparison that helps emphasize the distinctiveness of Stage 6. The Ten Commandments are considered concrete moral rules, whereas the Golden Rule is a principle that is "abstract and ethical." An effective compliance with the Golden Rule requires an evaluation of a person's conscience and ethical principles. In Stage 6 the focus is on the positive aspects of behavior, the "thou shalts" rather than the "thou shalt nots." The person who chooses to act at the highest level of moral excellence will realize a sense of empowerment. The focus is not primarily on mere obedience to the conventional rules, but rather on feeling and demonstrating goodness and excellence. Just as the community volunteer experiences a "helper's high," which contributes to a disposition to do good things, so the post-conventional ethical person has less of a disposition to settle for a life less fulfilling.[31]

When John arrives at Stage 6 of the post-conventional level, he recalls the days when he was a new agent struggling to learn his job, and he recognizes that others in his office are similarly struggling. He takes time to teach them how to be successful. John does not keep a commission-sharing ledger and chooses the other participants for sales calls based on the expertise and talent they can bring to the meeting. He insists on abiding by the rules and the principles that his conscience tells him are the basis for those rules. Periodically, John takes time to reexamine his ethical principles to determine that they are right and that he is acting consistently with those principles.

The example of John, the maturing insurance salesman, highlights an important concept: Even the observer inexperienced in commissioned sales will recognize that the practices described beyond Stages 3 and 4 may result in reduced compensation. Such practices may even seem inconsistent with the underlying objectives of business and employment, namely to earn a profit. Nevertheless, ethically excellent behavior is not about measuring and maximizing personal benefit, nor is it about being motivated exclusively by self-interest. Rather, it is about living a morally excellent life. And a moral life will often require personal sacrifice.

> **" There are occasions when it is undoubtedly better to incur loss than to make gain."**
> — *Titus Maccius Plautus*

When John chooses to spend time teaching the younger salesmen, he sacrifices, at least in the short-run, time that he could be using to sell insurance and generate commissions for himself. The fact that these younger agents may someday feel the inclination to repay John by sharing commissions with him is irrelevant.

As an insurance agent assigned to a particular office, John could likely get by as an employee by operating even in Stages 1 and 2, although he might find relationships strained within his office. The negative consequences to behaving at the pre-conventional stages arise in large part from selfishness. John's behavior in Stages 5 and 6 is right and good because it is unselfish and because it contributes to the good of his society. Experience dictates that such behavior can alter for good the behavior of others, though, again, this has little to do with the measure of what constitutes ethical behavior.

An important observation about Kohlberg's six stages of moral development is that moving up into the post-conventional levels requires a greater ability to exercise moral judgment. Business codes of conduct are generally designed to identify conventional behavior. To be useful, such codes of conduct should identify the behaviors that are specific to the responsibilities of an employee,[32] and, of course, maintaining a high level of moral maturity requires obedience to rules established by the code. Unfortunately, however, many of these codes of conduct are not sufficiently specific with regard to the varied responsibilities and challenges of people in the workplace. Reliance on these codes does little to teach or encourage the sort of moral reasoning that is required in dealing with the many ethical decisions that confront a person in the various aspects of his life. Stage 6, therefore, requires an evaluation of conscience and ethical principles that goes beyond mere conformity to a code of conduct.

Another important observation about the post-conventional stages is that behavior within the highest stages is, unfortunately, rare. I have witnessed it, benefited from it, and know it exists.

An encounter with such moral maturity is difficult to forget. It is, frankly, empowering. Let me share an example.

In a public accounting firm where I worked at the manager level, the profits one year were less than anticipated. The result for me was a slight decrease in my compensation. One of the partners in the office, not even in my own department, ordered that a portion of his compensation be allocated to me and one or two other employees at my level to allow us to realize an increase over the prior year. His personal sacrifice was clearly an ethically excellent act. The effect on me was to build my own inclination to perform at a higher level of moral development.[33]

Albert Bandura's Social Cognitive Theory of observe, judge, and react

Albert Bandura has described a theory of human behavior suggesting that people act largely based on what they perceive to be the future consequences of their actions. Determining the future consequences requires skill in mental imaging. Immediate environmental influences are a lesser determinant.[34] To Bandura's understanding, people are motivated to act one way or another based on their sense of values. Their personal standards affect the evaluation of whether the expected consequences are favorable or unfavorable.[35] These personal standards are derived from and influenced by parents and others in the person's social environment - their work, church, neighborhood, and school.

Bandura sees that people go through a three-step process involving observing, judging, and reacting. *Self-observation* is the process by which people consider and compare their expectations of themselves with their current performance, and "can realize shortcomings and inconsistencies between their beliefs and attitudes and their actions."[36] Next, people *judge* their behavior based on the comparison of their actual or contemplated performance with their standards, their past performance, and with the observed performance of others. They also decide whether the perceived activity is worthy of their serious consideration.[37] And finally, people *react* to the perceived consistency between expectations and performance or anticipated performance.[38] A positive judgment regarding the consistency of the expectations and the perception of the action or contemplated action influences the actor to pursue the ethical behavior.[39]

My Ethical Choice 7, "Choose to be an Impartial Spectator of Personal Character and Conduct," emphasizes this same sequential cognitive process of self-evaluation, self-judgment, and reaction. In the workplace, as ethical dilemmas present themselves, the need for this process is significant.

Virtue ethics

Most college courses on business ethics focus on how to resolve specific ethical problems.[40] Students work through moral dilemmas using methodologies based on either a rule-based or a consequence-based approach. Each of these approaches has its advantages and disadvantages, but both of these approaches are limited. What is missing is consideration of methods of *avoiding ethical problems in the first place.* Likewise, professional codes of conduct are designed to define *what* constitutes ethical behavior, rather than *how* to avoid unethical behavior. A consideration of *virtue ethics* can supply what is missing for both students and working professionals.

Virtue ethics has ancient roots - Plato and Aristotle are its founding fathers. With the rise of utilitarianism and Kantian deontology during the Age of Enlightenment in 18th century Europe, this philosophy, which had prevailed in the Western World for more than two thousand years, fell into disrepute. Serious consideration of virtue ethics in the 20th century arose partly out of dissatisfaction with prevailing utilitarian and deontological philosophies that seemed to ignore "the virtues themselves, motives and moral character, moral education, moral wisdom or discernment, friendship and family relationships, a deep concept of happiness, and the role of the emotions in our moral life."[41]

Virtue ethics, then, is a system of thought that focuses on determining how people should live their lives if they wish to avoid many of the ethical dilemmas that occur in the business world and in their personal lives. It has as its primary focus ethical excellence.[42] Virtue ethics does not identify all the rules and principles that would be useful to solve ethical quandaries. Rather, it attempts to identify the character traits people should exhibit in their relationships with others.[43] Virtue ethics is primarily concerned with individual moral development and goodness, rather than with how to resolve moral dilemmas.[44]

Virtue ethics considers how persons view, interpret, and prioritize the facts associated with ethical dilemmas and asks the questions "What sort of person am I shaping, and what sort of organization am I shaping by this proposed decision or policy?"[45] Because ethical dilemmas often require prioritizing the facts and the principles, virtue ethics considers how people value the elements of the dilemmas.

Virtue ethics has a positive focus; it is concerned with doing good rather than just refraining from doing bad. The focus of virtue ethics is the betterment of humankind, rather than the advancement of one person.[46] To that end, personal, voluntary sacrifice is sometimes expected. Virtue ethics encourages the self-examination of individual moral character and encourages improvement toward goodness.[47]

Excellent ethical behavior makes its own unique contribution to the workplace and in other business relationships by contributing to order, camaraderie, and trust. Among the most important of these contributions are efficiencies associated with trust. Once established, trust allows people to spend less effort on verifying the truth.

Virtue ethics is a demand for excellence, emphasizing *what* constitutes virtue and goodness within a human being. Excellence is not just superior proficiency; it includes goodness for its own sake. According to virtue ethics, inner peace occurs when a person lives a life of integrity. The focus of the *Ethical Choices* is largely on virtue ethics, upon defining the characteristics that people should acquire and encouraging the development of a disposition to avoid ethical dilemmas that are self-imposed. These are the characteristics that persons would want to establish within the culture of the workplace, as well as in all aspects of personal life.

Notes

1   Wallace F. Smith (Berkeley business school professor), "Readers Report," *Business Week*, May 4, 1992.

2   Donelson R. Forsyth, "Judging the Morality of Business Practices: the Influences of Personal Moral Philosophies," *Journal of Business Ethics* 11 (1992): 461-462.

3   "Idealism," *The Catholic Encyclopedia*, http://www.newadvent.org/cathen/07634a. htm.

4   Forsyth, "Judging the Morality," 462.

5   Oliver F. Williams and John W. Houch, *A Virtuous Life in Business* (Lanham, Maryland: Rowman & Littlefield Publishers, Inc., 1992), 18.

6   L.L. Jayaraman and Byung K. Min, "Business Ethics - A Developmental Prospective: The Evolution of the Free and Mature Corporation," *Journal of Business Ethics* 12 (1993): 667.

7   Jayaraman and Min, "Business Ethics - A Developmental Prospective," 667.

8   Richard T. DeGeorge, *Business Ethics, Fourth Edition* (New Jersey: Prentice Hall, Inc., 1995), 83-84.

9   DeGeorge, *Business Ethics*, 84.

10 Forsyth, "Judging the Morality," 462.

11 Forsyth, "Judging the Morality," 463.

12 DeGeorge, *Business Ethics*, 89.

13 Immanuel Kant, *Foundations of the Metaphysics of Morals*, 1785 (New York: Macmillian, 1990), 38.

14 DeGeorge, *Business Ethics*, 89-90.

15 Kant, *Foundations of the Metaphysics of Morals*, 46.

16 Christine Korsgard, *Creating the Kingdom of Ends* (New York: Cambridge University Press, 1996), 167.

17 DeGeorge, *Business Ethics*, 90-91.

18 Jeffrie G. Murphy and Jules L. Coleman, Philosophy of Law: *An Introduction to Jurisprudence, Revised Edition* (Westview Press, Boulder, CO., and Oxford, England, 1990), 78.

19 "Moral Relativism: Neutral Thinking?" http://www.allaboutphilosophy.org/moral-relativism.htm.

20 Gene R. Laczniak and Patrick E. Murphy, "Fostering Ethical Marketing Decisions," *Journal of Business Ethics* 10 (1991): 261-262.

21 Lawrence Kohlberg, "The Claim to Moral Adequacy of a Highest Stage of Moral Judgment," *The Journal of Philosophy* (1973): 630-646.

22 See a discussion of this issue, for example, in Carol Gilligan, *In a Different Voice* (Harvard University Press, 1982). Gilligan points out that Kohlberg's theory was based on a study of eighty-four boys whom Kohlberg observed over a period of twenty years. Some critics of Kohlberg's model have noted that many women who would consider themselves and each other to be mature would be identified by the Kohlberg model as "arrested" in Stage Three, where their moral development is "limited" to a level dominated by caring for and being sensitive to the needs of others.

23 Kohlberg, "The Claim to Moral Adequacy," 631.

24 Kohlberg, "The Claim to Moral Adequacy," 631.

25 Kohlberg, "The Claim to Moral Adequacy," 631.

26 Kohlberg, "The Claim to Moral Adequacy," 631.

27 Kohlberg, "The Claim to Moral Adequacy," 631.

28 Kohlberg, "The Claim to Moral Adequacy," 631-632.

29 Kohlberg, "The Claim to Moral Adequacy," 631-632.

30 Kohlberg, "The Claim to Moral Adequacy," 632.

31 Kohlberg, "The Claim to Moral Adequacy," 632.

32 R. Buchholz and S. Rosenthall, Business Ethics: The Pragmatic Patch Beyond Principles to Process (New Jersey: Prentice Hall, 1998), 177, as identified in Surendra Arjoon, "Virtue Theory as a Dynamic Theory of Business," *Journal of Business Ethics* 28 (2000): 160.

33 An observation of thinkers such as Carol Gilligan is that women, and even children, and many men, of course, routinely behave in such other-centered fashion, out of what a virtue ethicist might call personal virtue, or the natural or developed character trait of empathy, or generosity, or self-sacrifice. According to this line of reasoning, people would only have to "mature" into such actions because they have already learned some less worthy pattern of behavior.

34 Albert Bandura, *Social Foundations of Thought and Action, A Social Cognitive Theory* (Englewood Cliffs, New Jersey: Prentice-Hall, 1986), 19.

35 Bandura, *Social Foundations of Thought*, 240.

36 Larry C. Jensen and Steven A. Wygant, "The Developmental Self-Valuing Theory: A Practical Approach for Business Ethics," *Journal of Business Ethics* 9 (1990): 219-220.

37 Bandura, *Social Foundations of Thought*, 337.

38 Bandura, *Social Foundations of Thought*, 350-351.

39 Jensen and Wygant, "The Development of Self-Valuing Theory," 220.

40 Janet McCracken, William Martin, and Bill Shaw, "Virtue Ethics and the Parable of the Sadhu," *Journal of Business Ethics* 17 (1998): 25.

41 "Virtue Ethics," Stanford Encyclopedia of Philosophy, http://plato.stanford.edu/entries/ethics-virtue/#4.

42 McCracken, et al, "Virtue Ethics and the Parable," 34 .

43 Arjoon, "Virtue Theory as a Dynamic Theory," 160, 162.

44 McCracken, et al, "Virtue Ethics and the Parable," 26.

45 Williams and Houck, *A Virtuous Life in Business*, 18.

46 McCracken, et al, "Virtue Ethics and the Parable," 27.

47 McCracken, et al, "Virtue Ethics and the Parable," 33-34.

Text Box Footnotes

Adam Smith, "The pursuit of the objects ..." Adam Smith, *The Theory of Moral Sentiments* (Indianapolis: Liberty Fund, Inc., 1984), 172-173.

Henry Sedgwick "Moral behavior is far more..." Henry Sidgwick, *The Methods of Ethics*, (1907), 386-387.

Titus Maccius Plautus, "There are occasions when..." John Bartlett, comp., *Familiar Quotations, 10ᵗʰ Edition* (Boston: Little, Brown & Company, 1919).

Rejecting
Ethical Excellence:
Fraud and Deception

" The reverse of truth has a hundred thousand shapes and a limitless field."[1] – *Michel Euquem De Montaigne*

Unfortunately, unethical choices are commonly made. Ironically, those who make unethical choices, when their intent is to take unfair advantage of others, rely on a background of trust. At a fundamental level, deception presupposes and violates trust. In words of George Crabbe, "Deceivers are the most dangerous members of society. They trifle with the best affections of our nature, and violate the most sacred obligations."[2]

When people engage in buying, selling, lending, investing, and hiring they expect others who participate in these activities to follow through with their promises. When employees are brought into an organization, it is expected that they will learn their duties, show up for work, and act consistently with the organization's stated objectives. Employees are expected to refrain from stealing the organization's assets, revealing its trade secrets, or competing in a way that would be harmful to the organization. Customers expect that what they purchase will be consistent with what the seller claims and that warrantees will be honored when problems occur. Lenders expect that borrowers will submit

> " **The darkest hour in the history of any young man is when he sits down to study how to get money without honestly earning it."**
>
> – Horace Greeley

accurate applications and will make every effort to repay their loans, and that collateral is real and will not be disposed of without the lender's knowledge and approval. Without these basic understandings, the burdens of engaging in commerce would be too great to permit success. No amount of controls, due diligence examination, and monitoring can eliminate entirely the need for trust. Richard T. DeGeorge refers to this trust as "the oil as well as the glue of society."[5]

To understand the thought processes of those who violate trust, we may consider the negative extremes of the ethical concepts discussed in the previous chapter. This enables us to derive a formula for why people act unethically.

Moral Philosophy

The moral rationalist. The unethical person tends to view rules, norms, and laws as irrelevant, or at least as not applicable to him. His willingness to rationalize allows *him* to say, "That's not me," or "Under these circumstances, the rules don't apply."

With an eye only upon accomplishing his goal, he is willing to do "whatever it takes" to complete the task, regardless of other considerations. This focus on "ends" sometimes requires "means" that are inconsistent with prescribed behavioral codes or conventional practices.

The anti-idealist. The unethical person tends to view choices in terms of "What's in it for me?" He defends his self-interested pursuits with common justifications: "Let the buyer beware." "It's a dog-eat-dog world out there, so you have to look out for yourself." "Everybody's doing it." "They won't miss it." "If I do whatever it takes to save the company, everybody else will be better off in the long run." Others will help him accomplish his task, and he feels fine about that. As long as his subordinates are drawing a paycheck and are under his supervision, they must be loyal to him. He will decide what is best.

Moral Development Level

The unethical person functions at a pre-conventional level. He understands what is right and what is wrong based on the consequences he has experienced. He must make frequent assessments of the risk of getting caught. "If they can't prove it, and it is to my personal advantage, then I'll do it" is his rationalization. Short-term strategies dominate his thinking. Quite often, the strategy is so incomplete that there is no evidence of any assessment of the consequences. Investment schemes that are doomed for failure are typical of this form of unethical behavior.

Social Cognitive Considerations

The unethical person fails to spend the necessary time observing and judging before reacting. Gut reactions and emotions dictate his course of action. He may have had little or no positive moral influence in his home, church, neighborhood or school, and, therefore, his notions of what is right are different from the notions of those whose training and goodness lead them to make ethical choices. The unethical person has minimal concern with his level of competence. If he can perform the basic tasks and appear to be competent, that is all that counts. He is willing to rely on the representations of others, especially when the facts get too confusing.

Fraudulent Behavior

The ethical deficiencies described above are typically present in all forms of fraudulent behavior. Fraud embraces any form of behavior that has as its objective taking advantage of another through some form of deception. To simplify the discussion, here are the most common forms:

> **" Thou shalt not get found out is not one of God's commandments; and no man can be saved by trying to keep it."** – *Leonard Bacon*

1. *Simple thefts.* These involve the taking of another's property and can take many forms. Embezzlement, shoplifting, expense-account padding, robbery, and tax avoidance are some common forms of theft.

2. *Management fraud.* This activity is associated
    with creating financial reporting that is false and
    misleading. When avoiding taxes is the motivation,
    taxable income will be understated. The most
    common motivation, however, is to report earnings
    in excess of actual results. Financial managers may
    record revenues before they are earned, overstate
    ending inventories (which translates to overstated
    earnings), defer expenses, and fail to write off
    assets that have less than their stated values.

3. *Investment schemes.* These frauds involve solicitations
    of investments in which false promises are made
    of unusual returns on amounts invested, or they
    can take the form of illegal multi-level marketing
    schemes.

Simple thefts

Simple thefts appear in many forms, such as the retail employee who steals inventory, the shoplifter who takes merchandise, and the business person who submits a false expense report. Opportunities for such thefts abound. On a recent business trip, I caught a taxi cab for a ride to the airport. The cab driver offered me two blank receipts. When I arrived at my home airport, I prepaid my parking with a credit card. I was given a credit card receipt and then asked if I would also like a cash receipt. Why? So, if I chose, I could pad my expense report.

According to the 2003 National Retail Security Survey, $33.6 billion in inventory was stolen from retailers in the United

States in one year. Of that amount, $15.8 billion (47 percent) was stolen by the employees of those retailers. The inclination for people to steal from their employers seems to be increasing. One national survey determined that 35 percent of employees have stolen from their employers.[4] The bottom-line financial statement profit effect of employee thefts and fraud is about $2,000 per employee per year.[5]

Management fraud

Pressures to report favorable operating results have contributed to some of the more famous cases of fraud in recent times. WorldCom and Enron are notorious examples. The need to manipulate earnings can originate from pressure to preserve shareholder wealth or to generate more favorable bonuses to corporate executives.

Occasionally, the unethical activities of a business entity are so egregious that the business entity can be identified as a fraudulent enterprise. One of the most famous examples of a dishonest entity is Barry Minkow's ZZZZ Best carpet cleaning and damage restoration

"The great masses of the people. . . will more easily fall victims to a great lie than to a small one."– *Adolph Hitler*

company. At age nineteen, Barry Minkow began establishing outlets of his ZZZZ Best business throughout Southern California.[6] The real growth in the revenues and profits of Barry's business appeared to come from an outgrowth of one aspect of his carpet cleaning services, the insurance restoration business. Minkow claimed that he had established a relationship with Tom Padgett, a former insurance adjuster, who had connections with certain of the major insurance companies. When commercial properties, particularly large office buildings, suffered flood or fire damage, Padgett would contract with Minkow to perform the clean-up and restoration work. Why Minkow? His people had the experience and could get on to the site faster than others, thereby minimizing the water damage problems. In fact, only an insignificant amount of insurance restoration business was ever done by Minkow's company, and none of it came through Padgett.

Minkow learned that, in order to borrow money successfully from financial institutions and then go public, he needed audited financial statements. His first such "audited" financials were, in fact, creations of his associate, Mark Morze, who had kept books for various clients. The ZZZZ Best audited statements presented such a challenge that Morze had to consult accounting text books at his local college library to figure out how to prepare them.

Once auditing procedures became necessary, so did the fabrication of detailed worksheets and the underlying documents such as checks and bank statements. Morze became the master forger. He was so good, in fact, that at his deposition years later, even he had a difficult time distinguishing between real documents and his forgeries. Minkow would tell others he had a new $6 million restoration project, and Morze would have to fabricate the documents necessary to "prove" the project. He created his documents at home, where he had photocopiers, typewriters with different fonts, and a computer. Morze followed a logical sequence. To prove that money was coming in from the job, he would have to first create a real deposit, usually an intercompany transfer of cash. Each deposit would then be followed up by the creation of documents that would support false entries as to the source and nature of the transactions.

Morze used more than 100 interbank transfers between ZZZZ Best accounts in order to create the appearance of income. Later, fearing audit discovery, he discontinued that practice and began using his creation, Marbil Management. Disbursements supporting bank statement transactions were then created, followed by invoices and shipping documents. As a former bookkeeper for dozens of other companies, Morze had a plentiful supply of documents from which he would cannibalize what he needed: bank numbers, endorsement stamps, and invoices. What he could not find in his own files, he would buy from other sources, such as office supply stores or a printing company.

If Morze needed a cashier's check, something he used frequently since it made for quicker transfers, for say $150,000, he might buy one from a bank for $15, take it home, and then using his Exacto knife on his glass-top table, turn the $15 check into a $150,000 one. For those documents he wanted to represent as having come from bank microfilm, he would reduce the copies, then expand them, then reduce them again. At his peak production, Morze could produce a check in fifteen minutes. When Minkow and Morze needed a more complicated document drafted, they would hire a lawyer.

Outside accountants performed extensive audit procedures, including testing completion schedules, reconciling bank accounts, and sending confirmation letters to all of ZZZZ Best's outside suppliers. When the auditors, attorneys, and underwriters of ZZZZ Best demanded an inspection of certain of Minkow's non-existent restoration projects, Minkow spent $1 million renting large office buildings and completing construction on some of the floors. When suspicions arose regarding Minkow's alleged organized crime connections, an investigative firm was hired.

At ZZZZ Best, outside auditors thought they were confirming 100 percent of the suppliers of labor and materials to ZZZZ Best restoration projects. Some of those confirmations went to legitimate companies whose insiders - for a bribe - were willing to give the unopened confirmation envelopes to Minkow and Morze. Others were sent to post office boxes controlled by the ZZZZ Best principals. Minkow and Morze would then fill out the confirmations to agree with their falsified books and records and send them on to the auditors.

At ZZZZ Best, Minkow and Morze were subjected to days of significant interrogation at "all hands meetings." At these meetings lawyers, accountants, and underwriters involved in the ZZZZ Best public offering would ask Minkow and Morze questions about all aspects of their business. When these lawyers and accountants desired more

> **" The louder he talked of his honor, the faster we counted our spoons."**
>
> – Ralph Waldo Emerson

than verbal representations, they demanded physical inspections. A restoration job in San Diego was subjected to two such inspections, one after the building damage had been cleaned up and one some months later when the building was allegedly finished. The second demanded inspection threw Minkow and Morze into a panic. In a period of three weeks, working around the clock on three eight-hour shifts per day, they completed construction on two or three floors of the building.

Near this site and one in Sacramento, they set up a separate company, Assured Property Management, with all the equipment one would expect to find in a construction management trailer or office. They had blueprints made up. They even left less trash in the waste baskets for the subsequent visit of the outside auditors on the notion that, since the job was substantially complete, one would expect them to be generating less trash. At the Sacramento site, they pulled a building permit off the wall and altered it with ZZZZ Best's name. They left ZZZZ Best shirts and ZZZZ Best trucks at the site covered with an appropriate amount of dust.

Prior to the site inspections, they made dry runs, rehearsed small talk, and paid a security guard $50 to act like he knew Morze and to treat him like he was someone important. Morze prepared "a long laundry list" of items for Padgett and one other person to check out. As Morze described it in his deposition, they wanted the site visit to be a "tight, disciplined . . . rigorous plan . . . almost like [a] military plan." They needed to know distances and routes to and from the airport, places to eat, prevailing wages, and the local employment situation.

Minkow and Morze knew that the auditors and underwriters were not presuming they were "unquestionably honest." For that reason, they had to go to these great lengths to avert discovery of the fraud. To them, a $15 million public offering and an opportunity to go straight were well worth it.

Minkow was able to present an air of legitimacy by his associations with important persons and entities. He banked at substantial financial institutions. It is interesting to note that five of those banks discovered Minkow's improper check kiting activities. Three of those five just told him to

" **There are more fakers in business than in jail."**

– Malcolm Forbes

stop it, two told him to "take a hike," but none of them turned him in. Minkow befriended an official of Crawford Company who was short on money and long on authority to help Minkow by verifying Tom Padgett's background and the legitimacy of the restoration jobs. Minkow paid him $10,000 for that phone confirmation.

Minkow also recognized that there was benefit obtained by befriending the spouses of those he wished to influence most. He knew that when those people went home at night and complained about the problems inherent in being associated with Barry, he would have a friend "working after hours" to promote his cause.

The media paid significant attention to Minkow. He even appeared on the Oprah Winfrey Show. Certainly, he left an impression that he was on a fast track to success. He wrote a book about himself entitled *Making it in America*. After the fraudulent nature of his business was discovered, someone else wrote a follow-up, *Faking it in America*.

One of the behaviors most likely to arouse suspicion in a fraud examiner is when the person under investigation has befriended others such as accountants and lawyers whom he is attempting to influence. To influence his outside counsel, Minkow named his counsel's sons in his will. In an effort to imply legitimacy to his company, Minkow tried to influence the senior audit people by notifying them that he intended to hire a member of the audit staff subsequent to the completion of the audit. Among the "best affections of our nature" that Barry Minkow thus trifled with were trust, loyalty, and friendship.

The ZZZZ Best fraud was not discovered until a disgruntled person with inside information disclosed it to the outside accounting firm. Shortly thereafter, Minkow resigned from ZZZZ Best, and a bankruptcy petition followed. Twelve persons associated with ZZZZ Best were eventually convicted of fraud.

In 1988, at the age of twenty-one, leaving behind forever his Ferrari Testarossa and his mansion in Woodland Hills, Barry Minkow was sentenced to twenty-five years in federal prison.[7]

Investment schemes

Ponzi schemes. A Ponzi scheme is an investment scheme in which the enterprise earns little or no money, but the investors are promised, and receive for a time, returns on their investments that can only be supported by the subsequent investments of others attracted to the scheme. Hundreds of Ponzi schemes have operated since Charles Ponzi and his Securities Exchange Company made them famous in 1919. Most such schemes succeed largely because of the attraction of high rates of return. Most fail because their rate of expansion slows, and they collapse under the weight of commitments to investors.

In January 1981, Jon Con Vasilacopulos began a diamond investment business. Vasilacopulos represented that he had a direct source of diamonds through the DeBeers Diamond Cartel in South Africa. He further represented that he could buy diamonds at prices sufficiently low that significantly large profits could be generated in the resale.

Each investor purchased purportedly high-quality investment-grade diamonds. At the time of the sale, the investors were advised that they could take possession of their purchased diamonds, but they were also advised that it would be to their advantage if Vasilacopulos and Associates retained possession of their diamonds pursuant to a Safe-Keeping Agreement. Vasilacopulos could then, on behalf of the investor, resell the diamonds and earn a profit for the investor. Every twenty-eight days following the anniversary date of purchase, investors who left their diamonds with Vasilacopulos for resale could apply for and receive a 30 percent return. This return represented the so-called appreciated earnings on the diamond investments. Returns were paid, or, at the investor's option, could be "rolled over" and reinvested with Vasilacopulos.

Within ten months 3,300 investors had invested $13 million. When the inflow of new investor money became insufficient to meet the required returns to existing investors, the scheme collapsed. It was later determined that no connection with DeBeers existed and that much of the investor monies had been spent by Vasilacopulos and his salesmen.

A basic flaw in the Ponzi promoter psyche is that investor capital is treated as earnings to be spent, not as equity to be used as a foundation for the generation of future earnings and profits.

Potential investors often find comfort in the notion that many of these schemes have been subjected to the scrutiny of federal and state investigators. As with their money, their trust is often misplaced. More often than not, a Ponzi scheme will collapse under its own weight of cash obligations rather than as a result of a law-enforcement investigation. With Vasilacopulos and Associates, state investigators questioned the authenticity of the diamond investment scheme just three months into the company's existence. They even froze bank accounts of the company until they could, with the help of the company's legal counsel, determine that in many instances investors were, in fact, receiving stones for their investments. In truth, through the life of the scheme an estimated 400 stones, together worth approximately $1 million (if purchased from a wholesaler), supported $13 million in investments.

Multilevel marketing schemes. Millions of people worldwide participate in multilevel marketing (MLM) activities to promote the sale of almost any product imaginable. These organizations are a well-known "direct marketing" means of selling makeup, household products, and nutritional supplements. An MLM approach to the distribution of a product or service can be an ethical method of conducting business. Too often, however, MLM methodologies create a game of chance, in which the last participants inevitably come out losers. Instead of a direct marketing method of distribution, the result is a multilevel-marketing scheme.

In an MLM scheme, the primary focus of the activity is recruitment rather than the distribution of a valuable product at a fair price. The inexperienced sales persons of an MLM scheme are typically encouraged in their initial sales efforts to target their families and friends, who are inclined to buy as a demonstration of loyalty to their loved ones. Many of the participants in these schemes realize little or no success in recruiting beyond their friends and family.

In an MLM scheme, the significant rewards come from participants who are far enough downline from the upper-level participants that those reaping the rewards have little or no contact with or control over the lower-level participant activities. An MLM scheme is destined to fail because no market can be big enough to insure the rewards suggested by the promoters of the scheme.

Multiple factors contribute to the determination of whether an MLM activity is a legitimate distribution method or a mere recruitment scheme. Among these factors is the measurement of the fair value of the goods or services as compared with the price charged for them. In an MLM scheme, the actual value of the product is often significantly less than the amounts paid for it because significant commissions at many levels must be built into the model. Rationalization of the value of the product is typical. Under certain circumstances, real value exists, but on average usage, the perceived value is not realized.

I once investigated a multilevel marketing scheme where the product being sold was silver coins. The acquisition price through the multilevel marketing scheme was $28 per coin. The same coins could be purchased in large quantities at almost any local coin shop at that time for about $6 per coin. The promises made by the promoters of this scheme were unrealistic, since the "pool" of persons inclined to participate in this type of investment opportunity quickly runs out.

Another factor that suggests a recruitment focus is when the motivation for participation in the scheme is based on unrealistic expectations of earnings. Participants in an MLM scheme are almost always lured into their involvement by promises of big earnings with little effort. While most of the promoters of these schemes are careful not to suggest specific earnings potential, they utilize promotional hooks. "Do you know any people who would like to double their incomes?" "We have people in our organization who are going to do extremely, extremely well." "This program is much more valuable than a brand new Mercedes." "Who do you know in your area that's sharp and would like to make some serious money?" "Do you make 1k to 7k per week? Call _____." "Want to earn money while you sleep?"

Proponents of these schemes can identify participants who have been fabulously successful. Nevertheless, the test of whether any pyramid operation is proper is not in whether it produces some winners but whether it steadily produces profit for all. And the reality is that a very small percentage of MLM scheme participants ever make the sort of money that the lure suggests is available, and even this "success" is based in large part on failures of those below the winners in the pyramid. The proponents of these schemes suggest that the opportunities for success are available to all, and yet they have to admit that survival of the scheme is dependant on the failures of many at the lower levels; otherwise, market saturation would bring the operation to a quick demise.

The promoters of the scheme generally do not disclose the statistical analysis of the scheme in terms of average earnings, but instead emphasize the success of the few at the top of the pyramid. One of the legitimate MLMs, on the other hand, requires its distributors to disclose the average monthly earnings per distributor each time they recruit a new sales associate. Indeed, until saturation is achieved, significant economic success is possible with direct distribution methods, but since all pyramid schemes are destined to fail, even in the best of the MLMs the success of those who have the skills and put forth the efforts is achieved "off the backs" of the numerous others who will fail in the process. As the federal court held in one case, success is dependant upon "blinding potential prospects to the realities of the scheme."[8]

One of the inherent problems of an MLM distribution plan is in the inability to predict at what point the demand for the product will be saturated. In an MLM operation, there is no one within the organization with responsibility to determine how much is "enough." Instead, the sales continue to unsophisticated, inexperienced, new recruits who have the expectation that they, too, have the opportunity to achieve economic success, even independence, when, in fact, the market has become saturated.

The promoters point to unrealistic market measures such as the population of the United States who have not bought their product and "need" their product, failing to consider that a significant portion of the population will not be interested in either their particular product or the means by which it is being offered to them. The new recruits have bought into a false hope.

Some reputable companies using MLM distribution methods attempt to limit the "game of chance" aspects of their organization by placing certain limits on their distributors. Amway, for example, has what is known as a "ten-customer" rule. This rule provides that "distributors may not receive a performance bonus unless they prove a sale to each of ten different retail customers during each month."[9] Some, including Amway, limit the number of levels in the pyramid, usually in the range of three to six levels that can be the basis for generating commissions to the upline.

But even in the best of MLM ventures, failure rates are predictable based on saturation, skill levels, effort levels, and dissatisfaction with the product. And always, those at the top levels of the pyramid benefit from the initial participation of those who are destined to fail.

If the examples in this chapter sound a warning, they will have accomplished my intentions. No doubt, thirty years of fraud investigation may have made me more sensitive than the average person to the possibilities of the existence of fraudulent behaviors in the business world. Nevertheless, based on the ever-increasing prominence of such problems, and the fact that an increasing number of us seem to be affected by these schemes, the warning seems timely and, I hope, useful.

Notes

1   As quoted in Tom Morris, *If Aristotle Ran General Motors* (New York: Henry Holt and Company, 1997), 44.

2   Ted Goodman, ed., *The Forbes Book of Business Quotations* (New York: Black Dog & Leventhal Publishers, Inc., 1997), 190.

3   Richard T. De George, *Business Ethics, Fourth Edition* (New Jersey: Prentice Hall, Inc., 1995), 11-12.

4   PI Profiles International, http://www.AssessmentCompany.com/.

5   PI Profiles International, http://www.AssessmentCompany.com/.

6   The factual support for the portions of this chapter that relate to ZZZZ Best is contained in transcripts of depositions of Barry Minkow, Mark Morze, and Larry Gray. Each was deposed in the civil litigation brought by the class of ZZZZ Best security holders. Barry Minkow personally reviewed these descriptions as a further verification of the accuracy of the facts as presented herein.

7   Released in 1995, Barry Minkow is still shackled with slowly paying off millions of dollars to those he swindled. Now a Christian minister, he devotes his life to uncovering and dissuading others from fraud.

8   SEC v. Glenn W. Turner, 348 F. Supp. 766, 772 (D.Or.1972).

9   *In the Matter of Amway Corporation, Inc., et al.,* Final Order Opinion, Etc. in Regard to Alleged Violation of the Federal Trade Commission Act, Docket 9023 (93 F.T.C. 618).

Text Box Footnotes

Horace Greeley, "The darkest hour in the history..." Ted Goodman, ed., *The Forbes Book of Business Quotations* (New York: Black Dog & Leventhal Publishers, Inc., 1997), 409.

Leonard Bacon, "Thou shalt not get found out..." Ted Goodman, ed., *The Forbes Book of Business Quotations* (New York: Black Dog & Leventhal Publishers, Inc., 1997), 277.

Adolph Hitler, "The great masses of people..." Http://www.quotes.liberty-tree.ca.

Ralph Waldo Emerson, "The louder he talked..." Robert Andrews, Mary Biggs, Michael Seidel, et al, eds., *The Columbia World of Quotations* (New York: Columbia University Press, 1995), Number 21105.

Malcolm Forbes, "There are more fakers..." Ted Goodman, ed., *The Forbes Book of Business Quotations* (New York: Black Dog & Leventhal Publishers, Inc., 1997), 277.

Ethical Choices
Part 2

Choice 1

Choose to be Competent and Diligent

" Let each man pass his days in that wherein his skill is greatest."[1] - *Sextus Propertius*

Ted Williams played professional baseball for the Boston Red Sox from 1939 to 1960. His lifetime batting average was an extraordinary .344. He is the only player since 1930 to hit better than .400 in a season. In the 1959 season, he suffered from a pinched nerve in his neck. He explained that it was "so bad that I could hardly turn my head to look at the pitcher." That season his batting average dropped to just .254, and he hit only ten home runs. At the time he was the highest paid athlete in any sport. He was earning $125,000 per year. At the beginning of the next season, Williams was given a new contract that provided for the same $125,000 annual salary. Williams refused to sign it. He returned the contract to management with a note demanding that they reduce his salary by 25 percent - the full amount that it could be cut. Williams explained, "I was always treated fairly by the Red Sox when it came to contracts. Now they were offering me a contract I didn't deserve. And I only wanted what I deserved." During the next season (his last) he raised his average to .316.[2]

The baseball career of Ted Williams is a demonstration of excellence that has few rivals. Of Williams, author John Updike observed, "No other player visible to my generation concentrated within himself so much of the sport's poignancy, so assiduously refined his natural skills, so constantly brought to the plate that intensity of competence that crowds the throat with joy."[3] And there is in the example of his contract "negotiation" a peculiar demonstration of integrity that equals Williams' athletic prowess. The "intensity of competence" Ted Williams brought to the plate must have been the essence of his being. For when he found himself lacking, he knew he could not accept a reward he did not feel he deserved.

When one person is employed by another, the employee owes a responsibility to himself and to the employer, as well as to other stakeholders, to contribute the highest possible level of competence and diligence. People become competent as they acquire the knowledge and skills of their professions and employment and as they properly sort out the demands of their duties and loyalties. They then demonstrate commitment to these qualities by carrying out their duties with diligence and exactness. Developed in an ethical way, competence and diligence for such people, as for Ted Williams, are expressions of the essence of who they are.

Competence

People are sometimes critical of those whose performance, in their view, does not match the level of their compensation. Such people may berate the $10-million-per-year basketball player who misses a couple of key free throws or the baseball player who lets a ground ball roll

" I know what happiness is, for I have done good work."

– *Robert Louis Stevenson*

through his legs. While these criticisms may seem justified in the heat of the moment, they are actually frivolous, and mature professionals will disregard them. At the same time, however, competence demands continual self-examination, so that an employee or professional can improve his performance when it does not match his capacity. A person with an ethical focus understands that the true measure of his success is his personal competence and the diligence with which he applies himself, and these things cannot be based solely on the level of his compensation.

Anyone beginning a career that is at all challenging will learn early on that formal education has done little more than open the door to the job or profession. Knowledge in virtually any field of endeavor is expanding and

" It's what we learn after we think we know it all that really counts." – *John Wooden*

changing rapidly, and professional proficiency, today more than ever before, requires continual ongoing education.

Two-hundred-and-fifty years ago Adam Smith expressed this truth: "The prudent man always studies seriously and earnestly to understand whatever he professes to understand, and not merely to persuade other people that he understands it; and though his talents may not always be very brilliant, they are always perfectly genuine."[4]

Genuine competence, then, generally requires a significant, ongoing, personal investment in education and training.

Being competent implies having the level of skill adequate to perform required tasks. Wise young professionals will not be too impatient about moving up fast, according to what they think they may have the capacity to do. Instead, they will make

" If there is a single problem in business today, it is incompetence."

– Roger J. Sullivan

the most of opportunities to learn from the experiences offered during the early years of their career development, respecting and cherishing opportunities to learn from those who have already experienced what lies ahead.

Persons who are not competent in their professions and who undertake to perform them anyway often resort to cheating. Survival in a competitive world can be difficult. Pressures to succeed can mean the difference between having a well-paying job and being unemployed, or between making a sizable commission and going for an extended time without any compensation. Under these pressures, it is easy to rationalize that cutting corners or telling that "little white lie" is an acceptable means to accomplish a "worthy" end. Some people possess persuasive skills enabling them to "talk the talk," based on a superficial understanding of the facts; therefore, they make the sale, land the job, or secure the promotion. But those later affected by their incompetence can become the victims of their wrongdoing.

A few hypothetical but commonly observed situations can illustrate my point:

- An investment advisor is charged with the responsibility to determine the level of risk associated with investments and the appropriateness of various investment choices for clients. The advisor is deficient in understanding the financial performance of a potential investment and the trends within the applicable industry, but he gives advice anyway, feigning competence. In due time it becomes clear that the advisor's incompetence has seriously damaged clients' interests.

- A provider of construction services, a painter, makes promises to perform his work quickly and well. When the painter has too much work to handle himself, he hires others who are available but with whose work he is not familiar. The work does not meet the standards of the painter or his client. While the provider is a competent painter, his hired help is not. His customer is dissatisfied, and the poor workmanship of the job the painter contracted to perform is a reflection on his own lack of competence.

- A financial auditor undertakes an audit of a municipality. She has a great deal of experience in auditing manufacturers, but she has never audited a municipality. Her work is incompetent, and the financial statements contain errors that are undetected. Relying on the auditor's competence, others represent her errors as the truth, and

the effects of her mistakes ripple through the
municipality administration, affecting decisions,
policies, plans, and reputations, including, finally, the
auditor's own reputation.

Duty

When a person accepts the *benefits* and responsibilities of an
office or an employment role, he effectively accepts the *duties* of
that position. Unless he discovers that the requirements of that
job are morally improper, he should expect his duty to perform
as required to be a high priority. When a person fulfills his duties,
he is keeping a promise. Employees must be willing to set aside
personal preferences in favor of the worthy interests of their
employers. As James Madison wrote,

> Before any man can be considered as a member
> of Civil Society, he must be considered as a subject
> of the Governor of the Universe: And if a member
> of Civil Society, who enters into any subordinate
> Association, must always do it with a reservation
> of his duty to the general authority; much more
> must every man who becomes a member of any
> particular Civil Society, do it with a saving of his
> allegiance to the Universal Sovereign.[5]

The Civil Society Madison refers to can be any association that is
organized for a common purpose. For the objectives of that society
to be accomplished, the members of the society are expected to

accept their assigned roles, to fulfill their responsibilities, and to provide the support that other members require. Many people find difficulty in accepting a subordinate role. This is especially challenging when a leader is judged to be unworthy of respect, or when someone in a subordinate role has had previous experience that qualifies him for a greater role. Nevertheless, when someone makes a

> " I long to accomplish a great and noble task, but it is my chief duty to accomplish humble tasks as though they were great and noble."
>
> – Helen Keller

choice to be part of an association, he accepts a duty that requires setting aside conflicting, personal interests in favor of the worthy interests of the general authority. An important part of the duty of subordinates is never to undermine, even in subtle ways, the authority of those with the greater roles.

This does *not* mean, of course, that duty requires or permits unethical behavior, and persons in subordinate roles should not consciously hide behind the notion that it does. During a recent investigation involving a technical accounting issue, I became aware that those doing the accounting were uncomfortable with the company's method and the secret way it was being

> " Men do less than they ought, unless they do all that they can." – Thomas Carlyle

carried out. Suspecting that what they were doing had the effect of distorting the operating results of the company, the accounting personnel made their concerns known in a meeting with the board of directors. The concerns were dismissed, however, since certain members of the board were among the company's largest stock holders and were interested in increasing the value of their stock. The accounting personnel reasoned that as long as the board members knew what was going on, the accountants had no responsibility to disclose their concerns to auditors and analysts. While it may be unclear in such situations who has primary responsibility for the acts of the company, it is clearly wrong to hide behind the notion that responsibility to disclose wrongdoing rests with someone else and then to let the unethical activities continue.

It must also be noted that duty does not lie solely in subordinate roles. Those who accept leadership roles likewise assume duties. The leader's duty, or ethical obligation, as it would be described according to Kant's second formulation of the categorical imperative, is to treat subordinates as ends, rather than means. This means, in simple terms, that a leader does not "use" his subordinates for his own purposes but rather regards them as autonomous beings in their own right, whose choices he must respect, and whose welfare he seeks even as he seeks his own. In my discussion of Choice 4: "Choose to Comply with the Demands of Economic Justice," I further describe the leader's responsibility to fairly distribute the responsibilities and benefits of this association.

Loyalty

In my discussion of the business practices of Aaron Feuerstein, I described how his actions evoked a sense of loyalty among the employees of Malden Mills. He paid his workers better than his competition paid theirs, and he provided them with the best possible technology and the best possible working environment. He even continued to pay them at a time when he had no need for their services. Feuerstein's employees returned the favor by working hard to provide a quality product in impressive quantities. Tributes to Feuerstein suggest an emotional attachment to him, a form of loyalty that motivated the employees of Malden Mills to perform consistently with their duty to their employer.

Loyalty, in its best form, can properly motivate a person to set aside personal interests for the sake of accomplishing something good, such as contributing to the success and happiness of another person or to some other worthwhile cause. To be effective, sincere, and lasting, loyalty must originate from a proper source. For example, loyalty that arises from a sense of pride associated with the production of a good product or service is more likely to be long-lasting than is loyalty that originates from the manipulations of the boss. Also, persons properly motivated are more likely to contribute effort beyond what is required of them.

Deciding who merits loyalty can be difficult, but it is one of the most important of ethical tasks. The objects of loyalty in a business setting can include employers, shareholders, friends, and associates within the company, unions or professions, and business contacts outside the company. Whether a person is acting in a management role or a subordinate role, dealing with multiple objects of loyalty can be challenging. Management of a company is placed in a complex position as it directs the course of the company. Management acts on behalf of those who own the company. Management must be alert to the many interests of employees but must also be aware that it is working with someone else's money.

Subordinate employees deal with a unique set of challenges in prioritizing the objects of their loyalty. Should these employees concentrate their efforts to be loyal too exclusively towards one object, they run a risk of making ethical mistakes. Consider, for example, the employee whose loyalties are heavily directed to his boss and only secondarily to the company. If the boss fails in his duties to the company, the subordinate employee might be inclined to assist in the effort to cover for the boss' short-comings. Such efforts are rarely in the best interests of the company.

In short, employees and employers alike should be prepared to commit to be loyal above all to what is right. Loyalty to company and to subordinates or superiors is due and proper as long as the company, the boss, the union, and the profession are engaging in legal, morally correct activities that are consistent with the proper mission of the business. Of course, the determinations of appropriate loyalties are best made when people are aware of activities and responsibilities beyond their own. Further, they should have an appreciation and respect for others affected by their determinations.

Misplaced loyalty may arise out of a desire to get along, to follow orders, to win the acceptance of others, and to be friendly and likable.[6] Any ethical association should allow its members to think about the correctness of what they are doing and to express their opinions in an appropriate setting. The supervisor who demands actions that are illegal or contrary to the worthy objectives of the organization, or who fails to consider the informed thinking of those within his charge, does not deserve the loyal support of his subordinates.

When loyalty is wrongly placed, it is not a virtue. For example, employers may seek to build loyalty among employees through financial incentives and threats or promises concerning job security. The resulting attachments may place employees in situations where they must compromise more important ethical principles for the sake of preserving their jobs. In such a situation, it is easy to justify wrong behavior based on loyalty to an employer.

Many successful frauds are carried out because of the incorrect notion that it is always right to be loyal to the employer. A real estate investment firm in Connecticut, for example, persuaded several of its employees to gather around a conference table to assist in the creation of fictitious investment contracts. To the extent that they were morally sensitive, these employees were presented with an ethical dilemma: Should they behave as their employers desired, or should they refuse to participate in activity they knew to be fraudulent? Those who chose to participate justified their behavior, in part, by their sense of loyalty to their superiors. These employees failed to properly solve their ethical dilemma because they did not identify the more important object of their loyalty - their principles.

A proper sense of loyalty requires constant testing of the rightness of the objects of loyalty. No one can set aside good judgment and expect to be right consistently.

Every employee has the obligation to assess whether the employer who provides his or her means of living is engaging in honorable activity. It would be impossible, of course, for every company to provide the very best product or service that can be produced. Every entity should, however, be willing to provide goods or services that have value consistent with their price. When a company fails to do this, those engaged in supporting the enterprise should be anxious to improve or to move on to a more honorable working environment.

An improper sense of loyalty often arises when one person solicits help from another - a family member, friend, or acquaintance - in getting out of a bad situation. The friend needs someone to cover for him in a way that protects him from the consequences of his own unethical or incorrect acts. Out of a sense of loyalty, the person solicited may be inclined to help the friend, especially if the likelihood of getting caught seems minimal. In fact, failure to help a family member or a friend out of a predicament could seem to be a gross act of disloyalty. Those who fail to act to protect family or friends in such a situation may be made to feel ungrateful or even lacking in love and devotion. It is easy to rationalize this type of loyalty as a form of loyalty to principles. Loyalty to family and friends does seem like a lofty principle. It can be, however, an offense to the even loftier principles of honesty and duty.

Most often, when ethical dilemmas arise, a loyalty to principles of honesty helps in making the right decision. Right decisions are more likely to be made when people are effective in anticipating how they will view their own actions once the emotions of the moment are gone and the light of day shines on their decisions.

Fulfilling Responsibilities with Diligence and Exactness

Anyone who has embarked upon a challenging career discovers early on that hard work is required for success. The difficulty lies in defining "success" and in determining how much hard work in professional endeavor is prudent. Someone has said, "No business person ever went to the grave wishing they had spent more time at the office." A responsible diligence requires not necessarily more time but more attention. Hard work means discipline, an ability to recognize what is most important, and consistent willingness to allocate time according to correct priorities. Some of the most important business failures with which I am familiar have been allowed to develop because people in a position to be alert to the problems have not given an adequate level of attention to their work.

The moral benefits of hard work can hardly be over-stated. When I commit to work hard, I am less likely to be subject to the temptations that accompany idleness and boredom. I increase my capacity for and competence in performing tasks I may be assigned. I allow myself the opportunity to assume new and more interesting responsibilities. And I am more apt to do good because I am more inclined to think of myself as a good person.

Exactness implies giving attention to a performance that is prompt, careful, thorough, and consistent with technical and ethical standards.[7] It also implies that attention be given to even the small details. While it may seem beneficial to mental health

" A man reveals his character even in the simplest things he does." – Jean de La Bruyere

to not "sweat the small stuff," such inattention to detail may produce sub-standard performance, inadequate for the requirements of the profession or the employer.

"Sweating the small stuff" is precisely what is expected from the lawyer, the doctor, the insurance agent, the accountant, and a host of other professionals. People want to feel comfortable that those into whose hands they entrust their health and resources will understand what is important to them and care enough to attend to their best interests. Should we not expect the same of ourselves? The stakes may seem different. Yet, as long as what we do involves commitments to others then the ethical considerations should be the same. It is a sign of character when people are willing to apply themselves in such a way that they get the large and the small details right.

Code of Ethics Guidance Regarding Competence and Diligence

From the professions:

Accounting: Article V: Individuals should "observe the profession's technical and ethical standards, strive continually to improve competence and the quality of services, and discharge professional responsibility to the best of the member's ability." "The quest for excellence is the essence of due care." "Competence is derived from a synthesis of education and experience. It begins with a mastery of the common body of knowledge required for designation as a certified public accountant." "Diligence imposes the responsibility to render services promptly and carefully, to be thorough, and to observe applicable technical and ethical standards."

Education: Preamble: "The educator, believing in the worth and dignity of each human being, recognizes the supreme importance of the pursuit of truth, devotion to excellence, and the nurture of the democratic principles."

Education: Principle II (Commitment to the Profession) "In the belief that the quality of the services of the education profession directly influences the nation and its citizens, the educator shall exert every effort to raise professional standards."

Engineering: "Engineers . . . perform services only in areas of their competence." "Engineers shall undertake assignments only when qualified by education or experience in the specific technical fields involved." "Engineers . . . act for each employer or client as faithful agents or trustees."

Human Resource Management: "Strive for personal growth in the field of human resource management." "Strive to make my employer profitable both in monetary terms and through the support and encouragement of effective employment."

Law: Cannon 1: "A lawyer should assist in maintaining the . . . competence of the legal profession."

Marketing: "Marketers should . . . meet their obligations and responsibilities in contracts and mutual agreements in a timely manner."

Medical: Principle 1: "A physician shall be dedicated to providing competent medical care, with compassion and respect for human dignity and rights."

Medical: Principle V: "A physician shall continue to study, apply, and advance scientific knowledge, [and] maintain a commitment to medical education."

From the corporate world:

ExxonMobil Corporation: "ExxonMobil Corporation aspires to be at the leading edge of competition in every aspect of our business." "We will consistently strive to improve efficiency and productivity through learning, sharing, and implementing best practices. We will be disciplined."

Home Depot: "Each Senior Financial Officer is . . . responsible to do the following: . . . Owe and fulfill the highest duty of care to the Company over any personal, other professional or third party interests."

Citigroup Inc.: "When we act as a fiduciary, we are committed to meeting these responsibilities."

Notes

1   As quoted in Tom Morris, *If Aristotle Ran General Motors* (New York: Henry Holt and Company, 1997), 205.

2   A. Thomas Young, "Ethics in Business," *Vital Speeches of the Day,* September 15, 1992: 725-726.

3   John Updike at the National Baseball Hall of Fame.

4   Adam Smith, *The Theory of Moral Sentiments* (Indianapolis: Liberty Fund, 1984), 213.

5   James Madison, " A Memorial and Remonstrance," October 1785, as quoted in William J. Bennett, *Our Sacred Honor* (Nashville, Tennessee: Broadman & Holman Publishers, 1997), 327.

6   James Q. Wilson, *The Moral Sense* (New York: The Free Press, A Division of Macmillan, Inc., 1993), 54.

7   American Institute of Certified Public Accountants, "Code of Professional Conduct," Article V.

Text Box Footnotes

Robert Louis Stevenson, "I know what happiness is..." Motivational-messages.com, http://www.motivational-messages.com/quotes5.html.

John Wooden, "It's what we learn after..." Inspirational Quotes.org,"World's Greatest Sports Quotes" http://www.Inspirational-Quotes.org.

Roger J. Sullivan, "If there is a single..." Roger J. Sullivan, "A Response to 'Is Business Bluffing Ethical,'" *Business & Professional Ethics Journal*: 15.

Helen Keller, "I long to accomplish a great..." James Beasley Simpson, comp., *Simpson's Contemporary Quotations* (Boston: Houghton Mifflin Company, 1988), 495.

Thomas Carlyle, "Men do less then they ought..." Brainyquote.com, http://www.Brainyquote.com.

Jean de La Bruyere, "A man reveals his character..." University of Alberta, http://www.cs.ualberta.ca/-brewer/quotes.html.

Choose to Establish a Legacy of Truth

" So far as the human mind can shake off selfishness and act from a sacred regard to truth, justice and duty, so far will men not only be virtuous, but fearless in virtue."[1] - *Sarah Josepha Hale*

Among the interesting characters populating the moral universe created by Victor Hugo in his masterful novel *Les Miserables*, one of the most exemplary is Sister Simplice, a Catholic nun who "in all her life had never told a lie."[2] Hugo writes, "The fact that she never lied, had never spoken, for any reason or without reason, a word that was not strictly true, was the distinctive characteristic of Sister Simplice, the keynote of her virtue. Her unshakeable truthfulness had made her almost celebrated in the community." As Hugo describes Sister Simplice, her virtue is reflected in her appearance: "Her smile was pure and her gaze was pure; there was no cobweb or any grain of dust on the unsullied mirror of that conscience."[3]

For Victor Hugo, "The lie is the absolute of evil. There can be no small lie; who lies, lies wholly. The lie is the devil's own face. Satan has two names; he is Satan and he is Untruth."[4] Small wonder that Hugo created in Sister Simplice an admirable character who has earned respect, even fame, from a lifetime of truth-telling. Honesty is at the very core of her being. It is a manifestation of her goodness. Those who know her are willing to accept her word without question. The goal of every seeker of ethical excellence should be a reputation for honesty like that of Sister Simplice. When people are worthy of such a reputation, they are fortunate to enjoy peace of mind, with "no cobweb or any grain of dust on the unsullied mirror" of conscience.

Some seventeen hundred years ago, the man who would come to be known as Saint Augustine of Hippo, and one of the most powerful and influential thinkers in the Western tradition, expressed his belief that "any lie, and any promise not kept, was a sin against God's gift of speech."[5] According to Augustine, the very purpose of human communication was to speak truth: "Speech was given to man, not that men might therewith deceive one another, but that one man might make known his thoughts to another."[6]

A Reputation for Honesty

A reputation for honesty is not easily earned. Hugo paints Sister Simplice as someone whose reputation for truth-telling was built over a lifetime. Such a reputation is not earned by mere assertions or representations of honesty. It is all too common for a person to attempt a shortcut to the benefits of a reputation for honesty by pointing to affiliations with or activities in religious or other community organizations where "good people" gather. Too often, however, this kind of attempt at honesty-by-affiliation is merely a crutch for someone who has been unable to establish a reputation for honesty through individual actions. In the course of developing a firm reputation for truth-telling, a person often has to be willing to make significant, even costly, sacrifices in the performance of business dealings. For this reason, a person's reputation for truth is best evaluated from a long-term perspective.

" No legacy is so rich as honesty."– *William Shakespeare*

The Power of Truth

The person who has a reputation for telling the truth enjoys the special confidence of others. Communication with such a person is simplified since there is no need to filter information based on perceived self-interests. A complex business transaction should be a cooperative search for the truth, where the knowledge of all contributes to the fairness of the deal and where reported results provide a legitimate basis for making management and investment decisions.

One of the most powerful consequences of telling the truth is that others are inclined to reciprocate. When someone demonstrates a propensity to act in accordance with truth, others know they can

" As hypocrisy is said to the highest compliment to virtue, the art of lying is the strongest acknowledgment of the force of truth." – *William Hazlitt*

expect to engage in business with this person on a level playing field, assured that both sides of all transactions will be operating according to a common set of rules. Most people will respect those who live by a standard that requires truthful disclosures and kept promises. Granted, there exist some people who claim to view honest men as "the soft easy cushions on which knaves repose and fatten."[7] And it is certainly true that dishonest acts take advantage of the presumption of honesty. For these reasons, the conviction to live honestly does not relieve us of the responsibility to test, audit, review, and question the veracity of the representations of others. Thus acting wisely, honest people need not become "the soft easy cushions" of those who choose to live otherwise.

Importance of Integrity

I have learned from my experience as an investigator a simple rule: "Fraud comes in bunches." In other words, when I find evidence of dishonest behavior in one aspect of a person's life, I am likely to find it in another.

In Choice 6: "Choose to Follow Through with Ethical Resolutions," I discuss three factors that commonly converge to produce fraudulent behavior: pressure, opportunity, and rationalization. If a person under pressure can rationalize a certain unethical behavior, the likelihood is that, as various opportunities present themselves, the person will continue to act improperly. It follows that if persons are dishonest in business life, they might be expected to be similarly dishonest in their personal lives. The goal, therefore, must be to act with honesty in all aspects of life.

Honesty in Personal Life

Opportunities to act dishonestly in ordinary life are considerable. Here are a few:

- Most valuable movies, software, and music are subject to copyright restrictions. However, because of electronic capabilities, it is common practice to copy and share these items. Doing so is theft.

- Because of the infrequency of detailed tax audits, taxpayers are somewhat on their own in reporting their income and expenses to taxing authorities. Many people reason that there is a level of "enough" or "fair" that does not have to be exceeded. To fail to pay what is required by law is theft.

- Payment of taxes is often avoided through trading services or by dealing in currency. For example, I once bought top soil for my front yard. I was quoted a price if I paid by check and a lower price - about 10 percent to 15 percent lower - if I paid with cash. Why the difference? The currency did not have to go through the business account and, therefore, was not subject to business or personal income taxes. Had I agreed to the cash price, I would have been cooperating in theft.

- In insurance claims, financial losses suffered from thefts and accidents and the extent of personal injuries are not easily verified. Claims in excess of a fair value of the loss are often made. When that occurs and payment is made, the person making the excess claim is guilty of stealing from the insurance company.

- When selling personal items through the newspaper classified ads, by the Internet, or by other means, it is easy to misrepresent the condition of the item and to command a price that is in excess of its fair value. By this means unfair advantage is taken of the buyer.

- In some financial dealings, people make commitments that require a future performance. As time goes on and inclinations or circumstances change, people may feel justified in not following through with commitments. Perhaps the deal no longer seems fair. Perhaps the person to whom the commitment was made is no longer viewed in the same favorable light. Perhaps the capacity to complete the transaction has diminished. These excuses sometimes lead to a lack of performance, which results, once again, in taking unfair advantage of another.

- Related to the previous item, people sometimes spend recklessly. When they do this and eventually do not have the capacity to perform payment obligations, they are taking unfair advantage of another.

Honesty in Business

The notion of "fairness" in business is based on a presumption that activities must be carried on in complete honesty. Unfortunately, the business world is all too well-known for the lack of honesty that permeates it, particularly in the form of half-truths. Puffing and bluffing are the norm in some business activities, which means that participants in such dealings have to sort out the fiction from the truth in what is being represented to them.

In the workplace there are many opportunities for *employees* to act dishonestly. The culture of the workplace contributes greatly to the way employees act in the given situation. Consider these examples:

- An employer offers flexible work-hour and work-at-home policies that are meant to accommodate persons who have certain needs, particularly related to their families. These helpful policies provide an easy opportunity for employees to over-report their actual efforts on behalf of their employers. Unless productivity standards are accurately set and strictly monitored, employees can falsely report their efforts.

- An employer requires a certain minimum number of hours of overtime each pay period. All employees are paid a standard overtime amount whether they work the exact minimum overtime hours or something in excess of that. Employees are expected to sign in and out on a register each day. For the early morning sign-in, the culture is to designate a time much earlier than the actual time of arrival. Persons caught by fellow employees signing in using the actual time rather than a fictitious earlier time incur the wrath of those who follow. Those who complain reason that if others choose to work the required number of hours of overtime, they can do so and make adjustments to their sign-out time at the end of the day.

- A company is so large that the efforts of its individual employees become lost in the activity of the business entity. Night shifts, for example, where standards of effort are not measured and monitored, allow some to relax, even sleep, during hours when they are being compensated for real effort. When supervisors become part of the effort to look the other way, the efforts to monitor employee productivity are frustrated.

- Most of a company's office employees spend a good portion of the day seated in front of computer screens. They appear to be busy, but their actual work is, in fact, interspersed with playing games, corresponding with friends, and surfing the Internet.

- Because of the difficulty in establishing controls over retail merchandise, clerks at a jewelry counter in a large department store routinely pocket small items of jewelry. (In fact, many retail companies of

all sorts lose about as much from thefts by their
employees as by shoplifting.[8])

- A distributor of high-tech equipment receives
  promotional money and equipment from the
  manufacturer. With the participation and blessing
  of their supervisor, several employees keep
  the promotional money and equipment. They
  rationalize that this is part of their otherwise
  inadequate compensation.

- An outside government inspector of the company's
  product informs a management-level employee
  that he can "make life easier" for the company
  if the employee pays him a bribe. The manager
  does this, from his own pocket; then, with the full
  cooperation of his employer, he seeks and obtains
  reimbursement from the company by buying an
  asset of the company at less than its fair market value.

The workplace also provides opportunities for *employers* to be
dishonest with their employees. Consider these examples.

- When a company decides it must make cut-
  backs in its staff, it eliminates those whose future
  retirement benefits will be the most costly to the
  company.

- A small company does not provide all the required
  benefits, such as overtime compensation, that the
  law requires. But because the economy is down

and jobs are difficult, employees are forced to accept less than what the law requires.

- A company is experiencing financial difficulties. It applies pressure to its employees to create false documentation to deceive lenders and/or auditors. Because of personal financial pressures, the employees feel they must stay with the company, so they go along with the fraud.

The *customers, suppliers, investors, lenders, outside auditors, and taxing authorities* of a company are likewise affected by the dishonest activities of those who control companies. Consider these examples.

- A company sells products that have known deficiencies. The salesperson falsely represents the quality to be superior to what it really is.

- The company's purchasing agent makes demands "under the table" of the company's suppliers. The purchasing agent tells the suppliers that if they expect to continue doing business with the company, they are going to have to make separate and secret payments to him.

- Investors are led to believe that a company has steady growth in its earnings. In fact, the company has been "stuffing the channels" of its distribution system by shipping products through its distributors that are not sold and counting the sales as if the earning process was complete. The stock prices go up because the company demonstrates earning capacity superior to its competitors. When the truth of the pumped-up earnings is learned, the stock prices fall. Investors who bought at inflated prices lose their money. Company insiders take comfort in the fact that their representations to stock analysts regarding future earnings include a disclaimer that there can be no assurance that the earnings projections will be met.

- A company borrows money from a financial institution. The company is periodically required to submit borrowing base certificates that limit the amount of funds that can be borrowed from the bank to certain percentages of inventory and accounts receivable. The company "manufactures" accounts receivable to artificially inflate its borrowing capacity. The company continues to experience the same negative financial results that led it to the practice of submitting fraudulent borrowing base certificates.

- The auditors are charged with the responsibility to certify the company's financial statements. The company has incurred a considerable number of expenses that, based on their character, should be written off as current expenses. However, the company needs to report income to improve its profit picture. The company instead decides to treat the expenses as assets. Both the balance sheet and the income statement are overstated. The auditors are persuaded by false documentation that there is future value in these assets.

- A dentist needs some plumbing work on his house. One of his patients is a plumber. The dentist does dental work for the plumber, and the plumber does plumbing for the dentist. No money exchanges hands, and so neither reports the revenues that would have been otherwise generated, but for the trade of services. Both save on their taxes.

Proper Motivation for Telling the Truth

In order for persons to be absolutely honest, especially in their business dealings, they must overcome selfish desires for improper advantage and be motivated by an interest in establishing a legacy of truth. For some, that may require a greater appreciation for the benefits of truth in connection with business activity. For others, establishing a legacy of truth implies that the motivation lies in an interest in living a life of integrity. A discussion about the practical advantages of the truth in business would be misplaced because ethical behavior is not about measuring the advantages of a course of action that involves telling the truth. Rather, ethical behavior is about telling the truth because it is the right thing to do.

The degree of a person's passion for the truth will certainly influence his ability to live by the truth. Confucius said, "Those who know the truth are not equal to those who love it, and they who love it are not equal to those who delight in it."[9] Aristotle similarly recognized the effect of a passion for the truth, particularly when telling the truth may seem to work as an immediate disadvantage. As Aristotle wrote in his *Nicomachean Ethics*, "the man who loves truth, and is truthful where nothing is at stake, will still more be truthful where something is at stake; he will avoid falsehood as something base, seeing that he avoided it even for its own sake; and such a man is worthy of praise."[10]

All who are involved in business need to appreciate that the activities in which they are engaged almost always have an effect on "other people's money."[11] Even if people can appreciate that principles of goodness and fairness require that they not cheat and steal, they sometimes lose sight of the fact that business enterprise has a real effect on the well-

" Truth is the most valuable thing we have."– *Mark Twain*

being of others. Business activity requires a great deal of teamwork, both formal and informal. Dishonest activities in business have a tendency to adversely affect the success of the economic activity. If persons appreciate the benefits of the economic environment, they should be motivated by their respect for the system that allows them to operate.

A Disposition to Tell the Truth

If a person expects to establish a legacy of truth, he should expect to reach a state where he possesses a disposition to tell the truth. A disposition to do something is an inclination to do that thing as a natural or a first reaction. A person who has a disposition to behave morally will not have to make an adjustment from natural tendencies in order to make ethical choices.

To develop a disposition to tell the truth when such a disposition does not exist is a difficult process and requires specific effort.

First, we must recognize that inclinations not to tell the truth are inconsistent with the level of virtue that we should desire for ourselves. Most of us believe that we are basically honest people and that a few "white lies" and an occasional "whopper," if the circumstances seem to justify it, do not count as departures from the rule.

" **The most notorious liar, I am disposed to believe, tells the fair truth at least twenty times for once that he seriously and deliberately lies.**" *— Adam Smith*

But those who desire to develop a disposition to tell the truth have to be willing to eliminate all forms of dishonesty.

Second, we should begin the process of correcting our dispositions by planting the seed of desire. If desire is of sufficient intensity, that desire can act as a force within us to cause a real change.

Third, we must desire a conversion to a state of complete honesty, not just a limited course correction. That can be hard work.

Fourth, we must remember that it takes time to overcome habits of dishonesty, and our resolve must be for the long term.

When persons have a disposition to tell the truth, they are less inclined to dwell in that dangerous territory between the frontiers of honesty and dishonesty.[12] Most feel they have a notion of where to draw the line. Practically, though, there are gray areas associated with ethical behavior that are sometimes hard to define, particularly those where alternative courses of action have significant, conflicting consequences to the parties of interest.

Challenges to Telling the Truth

Some practical challenges arise when a person has acquired a disposition to act ethically and sets out to follow the resulting course of behavior. Such challenges can arise, for instance, from the potential legal consequences of revealing certain truthful information. This frequently occurs in evaluations of employment performance, particularly as they relate to employee references. Because of the legal consequences of providing certain information regarding an individual's performance to potential future employers, the information conveyed is often scrubbed of facts that might be useful for an effective evaluation of a person's real performance. Many employers do not allow the release to potential future employers of personnel information that might be considered unfavorable.

Because truth should never be used as a weapon, it is often difficult to know when to hold back on the disclosure of a troublesome fact or how to properly disclose it. At the same time, much of this difficulty could be alleviated if we could all be willing to listen to the points of view and the criticisms of others without feeling threatened or taking offense, and to make changes when appropriate. Otherwise, we may find ourselves living in error and ignorance.[13]

All employees owe duties to their employers. In certain business or governmental organizations employees owe a special duty of confidentiality and are prohibited from disclosing certain matters to others outside the organization, even if they find it morally objectionable to withhold this information. For example, occasionally, particularly at the management level, an employee may become aware of a matter affecting the well-being of another employee, such as an impending termination. Out of friendship to a fellow employee, it can be a temptation to warn him of the impending change in order to allow him an opportunity to protect his interests. However, the duty owed to the employer demands that such information not be disclosed.

Not uncommonly, a member of an organization may determine that someone outside the organization would be well-served by the disclosure of a certain fact. A duty of confidentiality, however, may obligate this person to remain silent about the matter. As an example, many people within a company may have information that, if

*" **Straightforwardness, without the rules of propriety, becomes rudeness."***

– Confucius

known to the investing public, would influence their stock ownership decisions. In such a situation, it becomes a significant temptation to reveal inside information, particularly to family and friends, prior to the proper time and means for disclosure. No doubt, disclosure of this information would prove to be useful to someone, but to reveal it would violate ethical standards because it would give preference to a friend at the expense of someone else who would be willing to buy or sell these shares at a price that is either soon to rise or to drop based on the release of the information.

The Expedient Lie

Many are challenged in accepting the need to respect the truth. For example, in my line of work I often provide expert witness testimony in depositions and courts of law. The factual basis for my opinions and the opinions themselves are routinely subjected to challenge by opposing counsel. Unfortunately, in this setting there is often an effort to make the truth sound like something other than the truth. Those who make these challenges are often well aware of the truth, but deem it their constitutional right to suggest that it is not the truth. In fact, this effort is, as Stephen L. Carter termed it, "nothing but an expedient lie."[14] However, when someone intends to tell "the truth, the whole truth, and nothing but the truth," half-truths, exaggerations, and any other form of deception must be avoided.

The Honest Organization

I have worked in many environments where honesty was the standard behavior and in one where it was not. Further, much of my working career over the past three decades has been devoted to investigations of persons and entities that have participated in and realized the consequences of dishonest behavior. In these experiences, I have witnessed the dramatic differences between honest and dishonest working environments. In honest business entities, there exist feelings of trust, satisfaction, goodness, and collegiality. In honest business entities, people are motivated to contribute to the long-term success of the entire entity because the entity exhibits the same virtues that people want in their personal lives. By contrast, in an entity where dishonesty exists, the working atmosphere is influenced by incongruent behaviors, such as sarcasm, insincerity, selfishness, and disrespect.

Sometimes simple things can contribute to an atmosphere of honesty within a company and a motivation to participate in an honest way. Let me illustrate with a personal example. In February 1976, I entered the FBI Academy as a new special agent. Upon arrival, new agents were given a tour of the facilities. The tour included a visit to the men's locker room. There I noticed something unusual. The gym clothing, running shoes, and other valuables were held in individual lockers, but there were no locks on the lockers. The tour also included a visit to the dorm rooms. Again, although there were locks on the doors, the rooms remained unlocked. Later, in one of the classroom discussions, we were informed that once we reached our assigned field offices, if we were to leave money unattended on our desks, when we returned we would probably find more than we left. Why? Because others would assume that we were taking up a collection for some good cause and would want to participate. Imagine how that made me feel! These were people I could trust and rely on for help. This new environment was so different from anything I had experienced before. It seemed like this would be a place of refuge, a place that was so good that I would enjoy the environment, and, therefore, I would naturally be motivated to contribute to the goodness of the situation.

Exceptions?

The reader of *Les Miserables* will remember that Sister Simplice did not remain true to her lifetime commitment to honesty. In Hugo's tale, Sister Simplice is assigned to take care of Fantine, who is deathly ill. As Javert, the police-inspector, is seeking to capture Jean Valjean, he visits the hospital where he knows Valjean has been giving attention to the care of Fantine. While Valjean is hiding in the room, Javert confronts Sister Simplice. "'Sister' he asked, 'are you the only person in this room?'" Hugo continues,

> There ensued a terrible instant during which the trembling servant thought she would faint. The sister looked up. "Yes," she said. "Forgive me," said Javert, "if I ask you one thing more. Have you seen anyone this evening, a man? He has escaped from the prison and we are searching for him - the man called Jean Valjean. Have you seen him?" "No," replied the sister. A second lie. She had lied twice, promptly and without hesitation, in an act of sacrifice. "I apologize," said Javert, and bowing deeply he withdrew. Sister Simplice! The saintly woman has long since departed this life to join her brothers and sisters in the radiance of Heaven. May she be credited there for her falsehood.[15]

It is easy to overlook the brief departure from Sister Simplice's absolute honesty, given the extraordinary circumstances of her confrontation with Javert. It is appropriate to assume that exceptions to telling the truth should occur only in the rarest of circumstances. A careful examination of my thirty-plus years of involvement in many aspects of the business world has led me to the conclusion that in *no* instance was dishonesty on my part justified. The challenge is to eliminate *all* dishonest acts, particularly where the primary motivation is in obtaining personal advantage.

Code of Ethics Guidance Regarding Establishing a Legacy of Truth

From the professions:

Accounting: Article III: "Perform all professional responsibilities with the highest sense of integrity." "Integrity requires a member to be . . . honest and candid within the constraints of client confidentiality." "Observe both the form and the spirit of technical and ethical standards."

Education: Principle 2 (Commitment to the Profession) Item 1: "The educator. . . shall not in an application for professional position deliberately make a false statement or fail to disclose a material fact related to competency and qualifications." Item 2: "Shall not misrepresent his/her professional qualifications." Item 4: "Shall not knowingly make a false statement concerning the qualifications of a candidate for a professional position." Item 7: "Shall not knowingly make false or malicious statements about a colleague."

Engineering: "Engineers shall be guided in all their relations by the highest standards of honesty and integrity." "Engineers shall acknowledge their errors and shall not distort or alter the facts." "Engineers shall avoid deceptive acts."

Law: Cannon 1: "A lawyer should assist in maintaining the integrity . . . of the legal profession."

Marketing: "Marketers shall uphold and advance the integrity, honor and dignity of the marketing profession by being honest in serving consumers, clients, employees, suppliers, distributors, and the public."

Medical: Article II: "A physician shall uphold the standards of professionalism, be honest in all professional interactions. . . ."

From the corporate world:

ExxonMobil Corporation: "Honesty is not subject to criticism in any culture. Shades of dishonesty simply invite demoralizing and reprehensible judgments. A well-founded reputation for scrupulous dealing is itself a priceless corporate asset."

ExxonMobil Corporation: "The Corporation's system of management will not work without honesty, including honest bookkeeping, honest budget proposals, and honest economic evaluation of projects."

Citigroup Inc.: "Each one of us is personally responsible for maintaining the highest level of integrity and honesty in our sphere of control."

Microsoft: "Delivering on our mission requires great people who are bright, creative, and energetic, and who share the following values: Integrity and honesty."

AT&T: "We are honest and ethical in all our business dealings, starting with how we treat each other. We keep our promises and admit our mistakes."

Berkshire Hathaway Inc.: "Covered Parties shall behave honestly and ethically at all times and with all people. They shall act in good faith, with due care, and shall engage only in fair and open competition, by treating ethically competitors, suppliers, customers, and colleagues."

American International Group, Inc.: "AIG business records must always be prepared with accuracy and reliability. The details of AIG's relationships and transactions with those with whom it does business must be accurately entered in its books and records."

Notes

1   As quoted in http://www.enneagramtest.com/handouts/enneagram.
2   Victor Hugo (Norman Denny, trans.), *Les Miserables* (New York: Penguin Books, 1976), 274.
3   Hugo, *Les Miserables,* 203.
4   Stephen L. Carter, *Integrity* (New York: BasicBooks, 1996), 91.
5   As quoted in Tom Morris, *If Aristotle Ran General Motors* (New York: Henry Holt and Company, 1997), 45.
6   Hugo, *Les Miserables,* 203.
7   As quoted in Ted Goodman, ed., *The Forbes Book of Business Quotations* (New York: Black Dog & Leventhal Publishers, Inc., 1997), 409.
8   S. Silverstein, "One in 15 Employees in Study Caught Stealing," *Los Angeles Times,* December 2, 1989: D-1.
9   As quoted in Morris, *If Aristotle Ran General Motors,* 26.
10 "Nicomachean Ethics, 9 Great Books of the Western World" *Encyclopedia Britannica* (Chicago, 1952).
11 As quoted in http://www.creativequotations.com/one/2115.htm. Delphine de Gerardin writes, "Business is other people's money."

12 O. Henry said, "There is no well-defined boundary between honesty and dishonesty. The frontiers of one blend with the outside limits of the other, and he who attempts to tread this dangerous ground may be sometimes in one domain and sometimes in the other." As quoted in Goodman, ed., *The Forbes Book of Business Quotations*, 409.

13 Marcus Aurelius wrote, "If any man is able to convince me and show me that I do not think or act right, I will gladly change; for I seek the truth by which no man was ever injured. But he is injured who abides in his error and ignorance." George Long (trans.), *The Meditations of Marcus Aurelius* (New York: Avon Books,1993), 43.

14 Carter, *Integrity*, 91, 112.

15 Hugo, *Les Miserables,* 274.

Text Box Footnotes

William Shakespeare, "No legacy is so rich..." William Shakespeare, *"All's Well that Ends Well"*, Act iii, Scene 5.

William Hazlitt, "As hypocrisy is said..." As quoted in Tom Morris, *If Aristotle Ran General Motors* (New York: Henry Holt and Company, 1997), 26.

Mark Twain, "Truth is the most valuable..." Bartleby.com, http://www.bartleby.com.

Adam Smith, "The most notorious liar..." Adam Smith, *The Theory of Moral Sentiments* (Indianapolis: Liberty Fund, 1984), 336.

Confucius, "Straightforwardness, without the rules..." ClassicalLibrary.org, http://www.Classicallibrary.org.

Choose to Be Other-Centered

" **In vain do they talk of happiness who never subdued an impulse in obedience to a principle. He who never sacrificed a present to a future good, or a personal to a general one, can speak of happiness only as the blind speak of color."**[1] *- Horace Mann*

In *Letters Writ by a Turkish Spy*, a work of the late seventeenth century by a Genoese journalist reflecting the notions of the European Enlightenment, the story is told of a French nobleman who is carried across an arm of the sea by his extraordinary horse. Upon arrival at the other side, the nobleman stabs the horse to death. His reason? He fears the horse might perform a similar feat for another and allow the other to be similarly recognized.[2] The actions of the nobleman in this story epitomize the selfishness that can exist in the heart of a man who is focused on individual success without regard for any responsibility to benefit others by his example, his resources, or his effort. Ethical excellence requires a focus on the betterment of all humankind rather than a narrow preoccupation with the advancement of one's self.

The Common Good

The common good is an important goal of virtuous behavior. The utilitarian may say, as Aristotle emphasized, that individual human beings by "promoting the common good"[3] achieve the ultimate goal of happiness. A deontologist would say that regardless of whether it makes me happy, I must promote the common good because it is the right and needful thing to do. A virtue ethicist might observe that a good person possesses the trait of generosity toward others and is interested in promoting the welfare of all human beings to the degree to which that person is capable.

Regardless of the approach we take, it is important to understand that self-interest and the common good are not polar opposites. In fact, in a free-market economy the common good is in many respects dependent on the ethical pursuit of self-interests by its members. Kantian ethics recognizes that human beings exist in a society of individual members with personal interests and emphasizes the need to respect the interests of others. Ethical persons demonstrate a respect for others, consistent with Kant's formulations of the categorical imperative, by recognizing that they are not an exception to the rules and norms of society, that they must treat others as ends rather than means, and that they must contribute their best performance to the community. When these characteristics prevail, the whole of the society benefits, and the individual contributors and beneficiaries realize greater achievement. Without contributions to the common good, the participants are diminished.

The Economic System and the Common Good

Any economic system should be analyzed in terms of fairness to the participants. Adam Smith recognized that the success of the capitalistic system relies on individual actors pursuing their own interests. In Smith's view, as an individual pursues his self-interests, he is "led by an invisible hand to promote an end which was no part of his intention," and "by pursuing his own interests

" The city . . . is a partnership for living well." – Aristotle

he frequently promotes that of society more effectually than when he really intends to promote it."[4] For Smith and many other thinkers of his time, human beings were moral creatures in a moral universe. To follow the interests of one's deepest "self," was to follow what was implanted by Divine Providence, and was therefore the sure way to work God's will in the world. But regardless of whether the "invisible hand" is seen in terms sacred or secular, in such a scheme as Adam Smith's, value is realized as goods and services are provided, as employment and compensation opportunities are created, and as investment opportunities become available. By these contributions, the interests of society are promoted as the good man pursues his own interests.

The value of individual contributions to the common good can be illustrated by considering a simple society in which only two families exist, the Farmers and the Hunters. The Farmer family farms while the Hunter family hunts. The virtues of competence and diligence as a contribution to the common good are illustrated as the Farmer family raises healthy and extensive crops, which increases their capacity to obtain meat from the Hunter family. Likewise as the Hunter family develops their hunting skills and works diligently to obtain meat, they increase their capacity to obtain healthy produce from the Farmers. Both families benefit as each prospers in their chosen area of work. Variety in their diets contributes to their health and happiness. Consider how their simple society will improve when the Carpenters and the Bakers move in!

Suppose the Farmers fail to properly attend to their crops, and the yield is insufficient to satisfy the needs of both families. The Hunters still have a need for the Farmer's produce, but because of the diminished supply, the price the Hunters will have to pay for the produce will likely increase. Both families are worse off. As the Farmers and Hunters recognize their interdependence, they will have no inclination to harm each other. Rather, their interest in being happy will drive them to help and support each other's best interests. As long as pride and jealousy do not enter into the picture, they will peacefully coexist.

Enter the Carpenters and the Bakers. The Farmers and the Hunters have been successful in working in a cooperative fashion. Their society was small and uncomplicated, but now they are dealing with people who are not familiar with "the way things are." Because the Carpenters and the Bakers have chosen to join the society of the Farmers and the Hunters, if the Farmers and the Hunters wish to be ethical, they must learn to be inclusive.

Philosopher Tom Morris has explained,

The history of human ethical enlightenment
is the history of increasing inclusivity. We have
reason to believe that early in human history,
moral obligations and relations were thought to
hold only within the family or within a tribe of
families. Anyone outside the tribe, a stranger, was a
threat and an enemy or, worse yet, a "nonperson,"
not even recognized as having any status in the
distinctively moral realm at all. Human moral
awakening has consisted in part in extending that
sphere of concern across artificial boundaries, as
well as beyond natural boundaries.

The greatest challenge we face nowadays in our
intricately interconnected world society is to be
truly universal in our ethical concerns. And ethical
tribalism, in various manifestations, is one of the
greatest dangers in corporate life today. Whenever
goodness is established within an inner circle,
it must then serve as a foundation for building
outward, extending that goodness as far as possible
throughout all the relationships in which we stand.[5]

The Farmers and the Hunters have an ethical obligation to
deal fairly with the Carpenters and the Bakers. Those same
principles that dictated their business dealings in their smaller
society now apply on a broader scale.

Business and the Community

Business makes an important contribution to the community. Business provides opportunities for employment for the local citizens. As it builds facilities and generates profits, it contributes taxes to help support the public sector. Business has an ethical obligation to the local community to compete fairly and to honor its commitments to its employees, customers, vendors, lenders, and taxing agencies. The public sector works to support local business by providing facilities such as roads and schools and services such as police, fire fighters, and utilities that enable businesses to operate in communities where people can live.

" A great society is a society in which its men of business think greatly of their functions."
– Alfred North Whitehead

While the primary responsibility for business is to earn a profit so that it can continue to exist, there are other important roles business can contribute for the betterment of the community. It can support the local business-promoting activities, sponsor athletic programs, and keep a section of the local highway free of litter. In my view, participation in these activities should be encouraged as an expression of appreciation to the community. But, again, in a free society, those roles are secondary and largely optional and should never interfere with the company's ability to meet their contractual obligations to shareholders and creditors. Anything that impairs the business entity from fulfilling its larger roles should not be viewed as ethically excellent.

Other-Centeredness

Roman emperor Marcus Aurelius offered some clever advice regarding how people should approach the day as it relates to dealings with others.

> Begin the morning by saying to thyself, I shall meet with the busybody, the ungrateful, arrogant, deceitful, envious, unsocial. All these things happen to them by reason of their ignorance of what is good and evil. But I who have seen the nature of the good that it is beautiful and of the bad that it is ugly, and the nature of him who does wrong, that it is akin to me, not [only] of the same blood or seed, but that it participates in [the same] intelligence and [the same] portion of the divinity, I can neither be injured by any of them, for no one can fix on me what is ugly, nor can I be angry with my kinsman, nor hate him. For we are made for co-operation, like feet, like hands, like eyelids, like the rows of the upper and lower teeth. To act against one another then is contrary to nature; and it is acting against one another to be vexed and to turn away.[6]

When people are other-centered, they accept that their obligations to act morally in regards to others are not restricted to those of their innermost circle of associates. According to the Stoics, "man was a citizen of the world."[7] Family ties and religious, racial, and national identities were not boundaries or barriers that restricted or defined ethical obligations. Moral truths were recognized as universal. All men had an equal claim for respect.

It seems logical that, except in instances where the right to that respect is lost as a result of the most offensive behaviors such as physical harm or defrauding, moral obligations are universal. This notion is supported by most of the great religions and philosophical systems of the world.[8]

> " **The world is my country, all mankind are my brethren, and to do good is my religion."** – *Thomas Paine*

I described previously some basic philosophical and psychological concepts that are relevant to any discussion of ethical behavior. I now return to those in considering the other-centered aspect of ethical behavior.

The Idealism and Relativism Scales

In relationships with others, ethical persons are focused on how they might positively affect the happiness of others, not merely by participating in the economic system, but also by engaging in activities that do not harm others and by occasionally sacrificing personal gain in favor of benefiting others. Harming others is an action that

> " **The good are those for whom undertaking the benefit of people is easier than undertaking their harm."** – *Plato*

highly idealistic persons would avoid at all costs. A focus on the circumstances and consequences of an action is, therefore, the natural tendency of highly idealistic persons. Likewise, they who are at the extreme, rule-based end of the relativism scale would also find harming others to be objectionable.

There is an important point here. Even those who eschew relativism may find that their humanitarian instincts can cause them to base their determinations of what is right on how they can provide benefit to others, even if conventional practices and sound economic theory suggest otherwise.

Let me cite an *extreme* example from the distant past. William Ames, an English theologian and mentor to the American Puritans, believed that it was a man's duty to lend to the poor and to expect no return. Furthermore, he believed that if a man met some mercantile disaster that did not permit him to repay an obligation, he should be forgiven that obligation.[9] The person who is *highly* idealistic might accept these unconventional lending practices as appropriate. They are certainly not legally based. The person whose primary focus is on rules and laws would find these lending and collection practices improper as they would contribute to the tendency of the recipient of the loans to be irresponsible. That person would reason that it would be best for the debtor to go through the painful process of finding the necessary resources to repay the debt. The norms and laws of society are rather specific in requiring repayment of debts owed by everyone, including the poor and the victims of economic downturn. However, the laws also provide a legal basis in the bankruptcy system for relief from most debts.

In my view, one can be a strong proponent of deontological (rule-based) ethics and still follow one's humanitarian instincts for the sake of others. *Sometimes* ethical behavior may involve relying on one's sense of goodness in deciding when it is appropriate to relax the demands of justice in dealing with others and then allowing others to choose whether or not they will respond with action beyond the standard that the law requires. In other words, sometimes ethically excellent behavior requires bearing the burdens of others, which might mean taking a personal loss.

Kantian Considerations

Kant's first formulation of the categorical imperative is "Act only on that maxim by which you can at the same time will that it should become a universal law."[10] When we are willing to comply with this law of ethical behavior, there is no need to make an exception for ourselves because the universality of the rules is intended to allow for equal treatment. Persons who are other-centered are eager to engage in arms-length dealing. They are unafraid of the consequences of the truth.

Kant's second formulation of the categorical imperative addresses the ethical considerations of dealing with others. Treating others as ends rather than means implies that we respect the dignity of others. We demonstrate characteristics of being other-centered as we are respectful of the interests and rights of others.

Kant's third formulation explains that, as rational human beings, we who act ethically understand that because we live in a community we are expected to abide by the rules of the community. That places an obligation to limit our activities if they may offend others.

Applications to Kohlberg's Moral Development Levels

In Lawrence Kohlberg's Stages of Moral Development, those who have matured to the post-conventional levels are particularly focused on others. Those who behave at the highest levels of moral development have a primary interest in the good and order of society. They have an appreciation for the good that the community contributes to its members and feel the need to contribute generously.

Delighting in the Successes of Others

The members of society are interconnected and dependent on one another to perform a wide variety of tasks. We all expect others to be good at and successful at what they do. Otherwise, the goods and services they provide could be unsatisfactory, late in arriving, or even unavailable. At the same time, some of us seem to have a natural tendency to feel jealous when we see others enjoying success and the rewards of their labors. Such an attitude, however, is self-defeating. Aristotle was asked, "Why is it that the envious are always sorrowing?" He replied, "Because they sorrow not only at any adversity that befalls them, they sorrow equally at any good that is granted to other people."[11] It makes sense, then, if we want to avoid such perpetual sorrow, to be pleased with the success of others. After all, the success of any one person contributes to the well-being of the whole of society. Of course, for those who are truly other-centered, it will be in their very natures to be happy at the deserved good fortune of others, regardless of residual effect.

> *"* **Mankind has become so much one family that we cannot insure our own prosperity except by insuring that of everyone else. If you wish to be happy yourself, you must resign yourself to seeing others also happy."**
>
> *—Bertrand Russell*

Volunteering

All of us have time and talents. When we are other-centered, we find opportunities to devote some measure of whatever we have to the common good. Let me share a personal example. Some years ago I was admiring the volunteer work that was being done by doctors and dentists to benefit the poor in my community and in certain developing

" **Few people do business well who do nothing else."**

– Lord Chesterfield

nations. I thought, "Wouldn't it be nice to have a skill that I could contribute in such a meaningful way." I assumed that accounting and fraud investigative skills were not easily applied to efforts to help those less fortunate. I was surprised when I was approached by the founder of an organization that provided free dental services to the poor of the community. He asked if I would serve on their board and contribute expert accounting advice. I accepted his invitation and was able to serve for a few years in that role. Sometimes it takes a little creative thought to determine how we can best assist as volunteers, but the needs and opportunities are numerous and will come to us if we are alert to them.

Those who engage in volunteer causes frequently experience the "helper's high," the exhilarating feeling that people get when they are involved in helping others. With such a feeling comes the sense of being a good person, one whose life is devoted to doing good. Engaging in activities that cheat or otherwise offend others will seem foreign to the nature and disposition of such a person. Volunteerism is a demonstration of willingness to sacrifice. Volunteering for good causes - for the right reasons - is a real demonstration of ethical excellence.

Choosing to Serve

In this as in each of the other *Ethical Choices*, creative thought and effort are needed in seeking opportunities to contribute to the well-being of others. My example of the donated dental services suggests that the opportunities can be somewhat hidden. A sincere interest in finding the right opportunities to help others may require effort.

> " **It is not enough to be ready to go where duty calls. A man should stand around where he can hear the call!"**
>
> *– Robert Louis Stevenson*

Likewise, with each of the *Ethical Choices*, neither the law, nor, in most cases, employers *require* that people perform beyond the standards of conventional behavior. A truly free society allows people to make personal choices consistent with their sense of what constitutes ethical behavior. In fact, there can be no truly ethically excellent behavior when moral action is merely conventional or compelled.

> " **Man was made for action, and to promote by the exertion of his faculties such changes in the external circumstances both of himself and others, as may seem most favourable to the happiness of all."**
>
> *– Adam Smith*

But if ethical behavior is not *required* behavior, from where does the motivation come that moves people to choose to be ethically excellent by contributing to the well-being of others? Most likely the source will be an individual sense of goodness, perhaps arising from religious convictions or from the examples of others, particularly when these examples are observed when a person is young. In the view of Adam Smith, human beings were "made for" the kind of behavior that contributes to the common good. Attending to and acting from our own best impulses, we will naturally seek to benefit our fellow beings.

Code of Conduct Guidance Regarding Contributing to the Well-Being of Others

From the professions:

Accounting: Article II: "Serve the public interest, honor the public trust, and demonstrate commitment to professionalism." "The public interest is defined as the collective well-being of the community of people and institutions the profession serves." "Those who rely on certified public accountants expect them to discharge their responsibilities with integrity, objectivity, due professional care, and a genuine interest in serving the public."

Accounting: Article VI "Service and the public trust [should] not be subordinated to personal gain and advantage."

Education: Preamble: "Essential to [its] goals is the protection of freedom to learn and to teach and the guarantee of equal education opportunity for all."

Education: Principle I (Commitment to the Student) "The educator strives to help each student realize his or her potential as a worthy and effective member of society. The educator therefore works to stimulate the spirit of inquiry, the acquisition of knowledge and understanding, and the thoughtful formulation of worthy goals."

Education: Principle II (Commitment to the Profession) "The education professional is vested by the public with a trust and responsibility requiring the highest ideals of professional service. In the belief that the quality of the services of the education profession directly influences the nation and its citizens, the educator shall exert every effort to raise professional standards, to promote a climate that encourages the exercise of professional judgment, to achieve conditions that attract persons worthy of the trust to careers in education, and to assist in preventing the practice of the profession of unqualified persons."

Engineering: "Engineers shall seek opportunities to participate in civic affairs; career guidance for youths; and work for the advancement of the safety, health and well-being of their community." "Engineers shall not promote their own interest at the expense of the dignity and integrity of the profession."

Marketing: "Marketers should . . . avoid manipulation to take advantage of situations to maximize personal welfare in a way that unfairly deprives or damages the organization of others."

Medical: Principle VII: "A physician shall recognize a responsibility to participate in activities contributing to the improvement of the community and the betterment of public health."

From the corporate world:

ExxonMobil Corporation: "We commit to be a good corporate citizen in all the places we operate worldwide."

Home Depot: "We will obey the laws and respect the customs of each community and will encourage participation and involvement in community affairs."

Citigroup Inc.: "We aspire to be known as a company dedicated to community service, taking a leadership role in every local community around the world in which we operate, and making each community a better place because we are there."

The Kroger Co.: "We will encourage our associates to be active and responsible citizens and will allocate resources for activities that enhance the quality of life for our customers, our associates and the communities we serve."

Notes

1   As quoted in Ted Goodman, ed., *The Forbes Book of Business Quotations* (New York: Black Dog & Leventhal Publishers, Inc., 1997), 685.

2   G.P. Marana, *Letters Writ by a Turkish Spy,* vol iv, Book III, letter 10.

3   Adam Smith, *An Inquiry into the Nature and Causes of the Wealth of Nations* (New York: The Modern Library, 1965 (1776)), 423.

4   Surendra Arjoon, "Virtue Theory as a Dynamic Theory of Business," *Journal of Business Ethics* 28 (2000): 166.

5   Tom Morris, *If Aristotle Ran General Motors* (New York: Henry Holt and Company, 1997), 140.

6   George Long (trans.), *The Meditations of Marcus Aurelius* (New York: Avon Books, 1993), 11.

7   Adam Smith, *The Theory of Moral Sentiments* (Indianapolis: Liberty Fund, 1984), 140-141.

8   James Q. Wilson, *The Moral Sense* (New York: The Free Press, a Division of Macmillan, Inc., 1993), 198-200.

9   William Ames, *Conscience with the Power and Cases Thereof,* n.p. (University Microfilms, Inc.), 211-257.

10   Immanuel Kant, *Foundations of the Metaphysics of Morals, 1785* (New York: Macmillian, 1990), 38.

11   Thomas Cleary (trans.), *Living a Good Life* (Boston: Shambhala, 1997), 25.

Text Box Footnotes

Aristotle, "The city..." As quoted in Tom Morris, *If Aristotle Ran General Motors* (New York: Henry Holt and Company, 1997), 102.

Alfred North Whitehead, "A great society..." As quoted in Tom Morris, *If Aristotle Ran General Motors,* 131.

Thomas Paine, "The world is my country..." Brainyquote.com, *http://www.Brainyquote.com.*

Plato, "The good are those..." Thomas Cleary, trans., *Living a Good Life* (Boston: Shambhala, 1997), 19.

Bertrand Russell, "Mankind has become..." As quoted in Tom Morris, *If Aristotle Ran General Motors,* 182.

Lord Chesterfield, "Few people do business..." Ted Goodman, ed., *The Forbes Book of Business Quotations* (New York: Black Dog & Leventhal Publishers, Inc., 1997), 108.

Robert Louis Stevenson, "It is not enough... Ted Goodman, ed., *The Forbes Book of Business Quotations,* 221.

Adam Smith, "Man was made for action..." Adam Smith, *The Theory of Moral Sentiments* (Indianapolis: Liberty Fund, 1984), 106.

Choice 4

Choose to Comply with the Demands of Economic Justice

" One thing here is worth a great deal, to pass thy life in truth and justice, with a benevolent disposition even to liars and unjust men."[1] - *Marcus Aurelius*

When a society is established upon the principle that the rights of all of its members are sacred, that society is said to be a just society. The members of a perfectly just society would recognize the benefits to be derived from such a society and would, therefore, be willing to cooperate in achieving their society's objectives and in sacrificing some personal gains for the sake of the benefits that are derived from that society. The members of a just society recognize that duties designed to assist the society must be allocated among its members, but the duties must be fairly and impartially distributed.

In a just society, rules are established that enable its members to understand appropriate conduct. The rules are not arbitrary. In a just society, institutions are formed that are determined to benefit the whole society. When disagreements arise, they are settled impartially. No one person has an inherent advantage over another; the rules apply equally to everyone. Rewards and punishments are distributed according to principles and rules.

All members of a just society are entitled to the same rights and liberties. However, in a just society, it is recognized that the benefits will flow unevenly among the members. The members of that society must not be unfairly inhibited in their quest to succeed and excel as they operate according to the rules of the society. Justice is not served if the freedoms of one member are arbitrarily taken away, even if, from a utilitarian point of view, the greater society would benefit from such action.

Each of these ideas regarding a just society is focused on the principle of fairness. These principles that describe a just society have particular application to economic activities. Adam Smith wrote of the "virtue of justice." He emphasized that exactness is required in complying with this virtue and that people should have a "sacred regard" for justice.

> There is, however, one virtue of which the general
> rules determine with the greatest exactness every
> external action which it requires. This virtue is
> justice. The rules of justice are accurate in the
> highest degree, and admit of no exceptions or
> modifications, but such as may be ascertained
> as accurately as the rules themselves, and which
> generally, indeed, flow from the very same
> principles with them. If I owe a man ten pounds,

justice requires that I should precisely pay him
ten pounds, either at the time agreed upon, or
when he demands it. What I ought to perform,
how much I ought to perform, when and where
I ought to perform it, the whole nature and
circumstances of the action prescribed, are all of
them precisely [fixed] and determined. Though it
may be awkward and pedantic, therefore, to affect
too strict an adherence to the common rules of
prudence or generosity, there is no pedantry in
sticking fast by the rules of justice. On the contrary,
the most sacred regard is due to them; and the
actions which this virtue requires are never so
properly performed, as when the chief motive
for performing them is a reverential and religious
regard to those general rules which require them.[2]

Economic Justice

The words "economic justice" seem to imply engaging in
transactions where the buyer and the seller are treated fairly. In
fact, economic justice is much more than just equivalence in
transactions. It refers to three principles: equivalence, distributive
justice, and contributive justice.

Equivalence

Equivalence relates to exchanges of goods and services at fair
prices. Equivalence obligations affect both the buyer and seller.
Of course, what constitutes a fair price is subject to debate.
From the perspective of a free market, an appropriate price is
determined by supply-and-demand factors. When the product

is considered valuable and the supply of that product is limited, the price for that product tends to rise. However, factors such as short-term emergencies and intense competition can cause unfair movement in the prices of goods.

Suppose, for example, that in the early winter a snow shovel sells for $15 at the local hardware store. This price has proven to be appropriate based on long-term demand and a reasonable markup from the wholesale cost of the shovel to the hardware store proprietor. Then a big snowstorm hits the community. Even though his own costs have not increased, the proprietor determines to sell the same shovel for $20, bringing himself an additional $5 profit per shovel. Because of the weather emergency, he will be able to sell a great many shovels at that price.

> " There are not many of us who remain sober when we have the opportunity to grow wealthy. The great multitude of men are of a clear contrary temper: what they desire they desire out of all measure; when they have the option of making a reasonable profit, they prefer to make an exorbitant one."
>
> –Plato, Laws

To the proprietor, the transaction is a purely economic decision. If he is going to sell out of his stock of snow shovels, he might as well maximize his profits. To the customer, on the other hand, who now must pay $20 for a snow shovel "worth" only $15, the $5 is a loss caused by the proprietor's taking advantage of the customer's sudden need. Is this a fair transaction? Demand for the snow shovels increased significantly, but was equivalent value given to the buyers? One survey suggests that most people would consider this kind of transaction to be unfair.[3]

A lack of economic equivalence can result from a number of factors. One party to a transaction can take advantage of another through fraud or duress. Differences in knowledge or negotiation skills or in resources and the strength of an organization may put one party - an individual or an entire institution - at an advantage over another.[4]

Equivalence also relates to employer/employee relationships. Employers are expected to provide wages consistent with agreed-upon terms. Employees are expected to work at a level of competence and diligence that will justify their wages.

Determining what constitutes a fair or equivalent exchange is difficult. Different theories of what is equitable can suggest different conclusions. Consider what is called the *equal benefit theory*. Simply stated, this means that what is given and what is received in an exchange should be separately measured, and if they are the same, then the transaction is considered equivalent. The *consent theory*, on the other hand, suggests that as long as the parties consent to the transaction, the transaction is fair. The snow shovel transaction is more easily justified under the consent theory, since under an equal benefit theory, the proprietor received a gain that was at the expense of the buyer. Under the consent theory, the significance of factors such as duress, unequal negotiation skills, and lack of knowledge of alternative choices - factors that tend to create an uneven playing field - are naturally minimized.

Equivalence imposes not only obligations associated with the establishment of a fair price but also obligations related to performance. The price established through a fair process obligates performance consistent with the expectations established when setting the price. Until performance occurs as agreed, the ultimate fairness of the price is not proven.

The system of distribution of goods and services is heavily dependent on marketing efforts designed to influence choices, to "hook" consumers into a decision to buy a particular product. Many of the techniques commonly used include characteristics of puffery. Consumers generally accept these appealing and entertaining "pitches" as part of the economic system. Without them, people would have less information, and life would be less interesting. There is little basis for condemning these efforts, unless they convey false information or clutter the interaction with useless but persuasive information. Ethical marketing is informative and is a useful means of bringing interested buyers and sellers together. It should not be an obstacle to creating awareness and correct understanding.

> **" He who fairly praises what he means to purchase, and he who enumerates the faults of what he means to sell, may set up a partnership with honesty."**
>
> *–John Lavater*

A basic rule of fairness in a transaction is that both parties should have adequate knowledge of the relevant facts so they can make an informed decision. What parties consider adequate disclosure depends, in part, on whether their perceptions are based on theory or on practice. In other words, some can point to a rule, such as the Golden Rule, that suggests a level of disclosure, while others point to their observations of how disclosures are generally made in the business in question.

Suppose, for example, I want to sell my car. Lately, my car's transmission has been making strange sounds, not all the time, but once in a while. I advertise the sale of my car in the newspaper, and someone comes to look it over and take it for a test drive. During their test drive, the transmission noises do not occur. It is my intention to sell the car "as is," and I will write that into the contract. Do I have an obligation to tell the potential buyer about the transmission noises? If I believe, and am willing to follow my beliefs, that the Golden Rule requires that I place myself in the shoes of the buyer, I understand that since the buyer would want to know that fact, I am obligated to disclose it. On the other hand, if I believe that the way used cars are normally sold is to "let the buyer beware," I can sell my car without disclosing the probable defect. Those who would argue that the "let the buyer beware" position in this transaction is proper, and that this condition is a risk that affects the price the buyer is willing to pay, might also argue that following the Golden Rule would be naïve and inconsistent with common practices. This example highlights the fact that relying on business practice frequently ignores the "requirements" of ethical excellence. When deceived victims are the end product of a transaction, the transaction is properly viewed as unfair.[5]

In 1888, Standard Oil Company executives were summoned to testify before a government committee. Their boss, Paul Babcock, an associate of John D. Rockefeller, instructed them as follows: "Parry every question with answers which, while perfectly truthful, are evasive of *bottom* facts."[6] The proponents of business bluffing would regard this strategy as permissible in business transactions. This strategy could hardly result in the full disclosure requirements of arms-length dealing.

Most often, the choices to be made are not as simple as to reveal or not to reveal some critical fact. It would seem basic to assume that the seller has an obligation to tell the truth when answering the direct questions of the buyer. Beyond that, the choices involve degrees of disclosure, and reasonable people may differ about how much disclosure is ethically required. At the extreme minimum lies the assumption that the buyer is responsible for his own due diligence in preparing for the transaction. Moving toward the other end of the scale, most would agree that the seller should disclose facts affecting safety as well as matters that the buyer would not be likely to discover with reasonable effort. The ethical seller might also disclose additional information that would assist the buyer in making an informed and reasonable judgment, until, at the extreme end of the disclosure scale, the seller would be expected to disclose everything he perceives is necessary to enable the buyer to make a good decision.

Decisions about appropriate levels of disclosure must often be made in the context of performance of duties. Salespersons have a duty to their employers to be advocates of the goods or services they are selling. They may receive specific guidance as to the disclosures they are to provide in their sales pitch.[7] Whether that guidance is consistent with a particular salesperson's ethical sensibilities is an important determination that each must make, since duties to perform are subject to limitations, both ethical and legal. While salespersons have a duty to sell according to the interests of their employers, ethical constraints would not allow them to sell products to those who do not require them. Examples abound of ruthless salespersons who peddle home appliances, repairs, and mortgage financing to those who have neither the need nor the capacity to make such acquisitions.

Professional and legal requirements may also affect the degree of disclosure. The Code of Professional Responsibility of the American Bar Association, for example, requires lawyers to "represent a client zealously within the bounds of the law." That requirement is not restricted to advocacy in the court room. Lawyers become involved in "deals" also. Their Code of Professional Responsibility would seem to restrict them from assisting the opposing side in analyzing their position in the transaction. However, lawyers must be fair and honest in their representations of clients, and in their business dealings as well.

It is helpful when considering appropriate levels of disclosure to refer to the American Marketing Association's Code of Ethics. The AMA's code includes this guidance:

- "[Be] honest in serving consumers, clients, employees, suppliers, distributors, and the public."

- "Participants in the marketing exchange process should be able to expect that

  1. Products and services offered are safe and fit for their intended uses;
  2. Communications about offered products and services are not deceptive;
  3. All parties intend to discharge their obligations, financial and otherwise, in good faith; and
  4. Appropriate internal methods exist for equitable adjustment and/or redress of grievances concerning purchases."[8]

Since the AMA Code prohibits communications that are deceptive, it would seem to frown on the idea discussed earlier that business activity can be viewed as a game where bluffing is acceptable.

Distributive Justice

Distributive justice relates to the associations of greater and lesser authority. Its primary focus is on the workplace, rather than the marketplace. In order to comply with the requirements of distributive justice, a person of greater authority is expected to be fair in the distribution of both the burdens and the benefits to those of lesser authority. This concept implies an even-handedness on the part of the boss in dealing with subordinates. Every employee under the boss's direction must be treated with respect. Decisions that result in uneven distributions of benefits should be justified by the most objective criteria possible. Abuses of this principle would include "favoritism and arbitrariness."[9]

Kant's second formulation of the categorical imperative has application to distributive justice. The second formulation reads, "Act so that you treat humanity whether, in your own person or in that of another, always as an end and never as a means only."[10] This "Formula of Humanity"[11] requires that we consider the dignity and worth of others affected by our action.

The role of the subordinates is not merely to enhance the career of the boss. It is a reflection of the character of the boss that he treats those in subordinate roles with respect, even when the rules and customs of the workplace allow otherwise. It would be easy to argue from experience that performance generally improves if subordinates are treated with respect. However, ethics requires respectful treatment in spite of the logical outcomes. Compliance with the principle of distributive justice would also imply that when subordinates achieve some success, they should be appropriately rewarded.

All persons who are in a position of authority over others have the responsibility to set the example of dealing justly with those whom they supervise. The "tone at the top" has an extraordinary impact on those affected by the leadership.

Failure of superiors to comply with distributive justice requirements is a frequent rationalization used by subordinates who engage in unethical behaviors. Stealing to compensate for unfair treatment is one such example. Similarly, disrespectful treatment of subordinates can lead to inferior performance that is viewed as a means to "get even" with the boss. As Tom Morris described it, "If we do not celebrate them in positive ways, they may be very tempted to celebrate themselves in negative ways, rewarding themselves with prizes that are not rightfully theirs for the taking."[12]

> **" Among the characteristics of a free man is that his patience in the betterment of those below him is greater than his patience in seeking the favor of those above him, and he tolerates more from those who are weaker than he tolerates from those who are stronger."**
>
> *—Plato*

Failure to comply with the principle of distributive justice is a reflection of insensitivity. During the early 1930s, Henry Ford objected to the idea of providing unemployment insurance to employees. He reasoned that unemployment could be a good condition. "Why, it's the best education in the world for those boys, that traveling around! They get more experience in a few months than they would in years of school."[13] Ethical excellence would suggest a more liberal distribution of benefits to Mr. Ford's subordinates.

Contributive Justice

Contributive justice relates to relationships within groups. When we benefit from a group, we have an obligation to support that group. Our chief obligation to the group is compliance with the ethical rules of that group so as not to discredit its other members.[14]

Those who fail to comply with the most basic of ethical standards can have a negative impact, not only on others within their organization, but more broadly on others engaged in similar activities. Sales people are generally affected negatively by those who use deceptive practices. Used-car salesmen are an easy target to illustrate this point. Likewise, consider that the trust and credibility of some professions, namely accountants and lawyers, suffer when the highly-publicized business frauds are disclosed in the press.

The Golden Rule

Each of the elements of economic justice - equivalence, distributive justice, and contributive justice - is associated with fairness in relationships. Most of the major religions of the world recognize the importance of fairness in relationships and include as a basic tenet a rule that dictates the need to act in such a way that the interests of the other person are honored.[15] In Christianity, that teaching has come to be known as the Golden Rule: "Do unto others as you would have others do unto you." Buddhism has a similar rule: "Seek for others the happiness you desire for yourself. Hurt not others with that which pains you." Judaism's version is, "That which is hurtful to you, do not do to your fellow man." Islam teaches, "Let none of you treat his brother in a way he himself would not like to be treated. No one of you is a believer until he loves for his brother what he loves for himself."[16] All of these teachings would clearly rule out engaging in deceptive practices such as accepting bribes, cheating on expense reports, misrepresenting a product, or treating an employee in an unfair way, since these practices are designed to benefit one person while putting others at a disadvantage.[17]

Properly applying the principle of the Golden Rule can present certain challenges. Acting in strict compliance with the principle, people naturally assume that what they think is right or desirable is what is best for others. However, differences in culture, need, and preference can affect what another person would deem acceptable. Say, for

> " **Friendship among citizens of an ideal state would make justice unnecessary, as friends do not injure but only do what is good for each other."**
>
> –Aristotle

example, that a male employer consistently makes what he thinks are flattering remarks to a female subordinate, paying her the kind of attention he would be more than pleased to have her pay to him. He is surprised to discover that she finds his attention offensive and intrusive. Or suppose that an investment advisor chooses an aggressive stock investment for one of his conservative clients, thinking that this transaction is probably in the best interests of his client and is consistent with what he would do for himself. Whether the stock investment turns out to be a success is irrelevant to the purchase decision. The investment advisor, like the flattering employer, has failed in his duty, since he has failed to consider that his client's or subordinate's needs and desires are not necessarily the same as his own. Such examples imply that a liberal application of the Golden Rule would require the ability to understand the preferences of others, so that people do not end up imposing their own preferences on unwilling recipients.[18]

Recognizing this difference in needs, someone has suggested a "platinum rule": "Do unto others as they would have you do unto them."[19] This rule is much more difficult to follow than its golden counterpart. But if we are truly other-centered seekers of ethical excellence, we will make the effort to discover, insofar as it is possible, how the notions of others about what is right and desirable for them may differ from our own ideas, so that we will not find ourselves imposing our preferences on others.

While adherence to any version of other-honoring goes a long way toward contributing to economic justice in relationships, it does not address all of the issues commonly faced in business relationships. Consider, for example, the sale of a valuable asset such as a house. Based on a recent independent appraisal of another comparable dwelling, the seller decides to list the house at $200,000. He is eager to sell, and expects that if a cash offer comes in at $185,000 he will accept it. Any interested buyer would like to know what the seller would be willing to take for the house. Suppose a potential buyer makes an offer of $190,000 but is willing to raise his offer to $195,000. Between the buyer and the seller, there is $10,000 of potential advantage. Had the buyer known that the seller would accept $5,000 less than that, he would most certainly have offered less. The buyer and the seller have competing economic interests. From the point of view of the buyer, if he wishes to follow the Golden Rule, should he be expected to offer his top price? And from the point of view of the seller, should he be willing to identify his lowest acceptable price?

The process of bargaining is a dynamic one in which neither party is obligated, legally or ethically, to disclose all expectations. In fact, if either of the parties was obligated to disclose bidding limits, that party would be disadvantaged in a process designed to determine the correct price. Both the buyer and the seller enter into this bargaining relationship knowing how the bargaining process works. As long as both are satisfied that the exchange was fair and open, the deal should be considered proper.[20]

Suppose, on the other hand, that the seller learns before listing the house for sale of structural problems, such as termites, expansive soils, or foundation leaks, that have a real impact on the value of the house. Assuming that there is no specific requirement in the contract to represent the house to be free of these defects, would the seller be obligated to disclose these matters? Absolutely!

From an ethical point of view, what is the difference between not disclosing the defects and not disclosing willingness to accept an offer that is less than the amount being offered? Arriving at a fair price through a bargaining process recognizes that persons who are fully informed may have differences of opinion that are affected by their needs and preferences. The willing buyer and the willing seller need to go through a negotiation process to arrive at a price that suits the needs of both. As long as both are properly informed of the significant factors indicating the value of the property in question, both are treated fairly. In this case, the seller of the house was anxious to sell as soon as possible. To the seller, accepting a lower price for the sake of a quick sell made perfect sense. The buyer saw value in the home in a range of $190,000 to $195,000. His interests were satisfied as long as the agreed-upon price fell within that range.[21]

Business decisions can have a variety of effects that affect different people in different ways. Suppose a publicly owned company has multiple manufacturing facilities, and one of their plants is losing money to such an extent that it is likely to take the whole company into bankruptcy if the losses are allowed to continue. The decision to close the unprofitable plant and lay off its workers is right for those

> **" Every man takes care that his neighbor shall not cheat him. But a day comes when he begins to care that he does not cheat his neighbor. Then all goes well."**
>
> —*Ralph Waldo Emerson*

with an interest in the survival of the company, but to those who are employed at the facility to be closed, closing the plant seems inconsistent with the Golden Rule. In this example, what may be the right decision has a negative impact on some and a positive impact on others.[22]

The Golden Rule is an important part of virtue ethics. As I have discussed earlier, virtue ethics is less focused on rights and duties than on individual responsibilities. Virtue ethics invites us all to focus on our responsibility to respect and preserve the rights of others.[23] To be dealt with honestly in business dealings is a right to which we all feel entitled. I have mentioned that some amount of puffery in advertising is common and generally expected and can even be entertaining. Business bluffing, on the other hand, is falsehood designed to secure advantage from another - to take more than would be otherwise necessary to complete an equitable transaction. Strict adherence to the Golden Rule would, therefore, seem to place any form of business bluffing securely in the realm of the unethical.

Code of Ethics Guidance Regarding Equivalence

From the professions:

Marketing: "Marketers shall uphold and advance the integrity, honor and dignity of the marketing profession by: Establishing equitable fee schedules including the payment or receipt of usual, customary and/or legal compensation for marketing exchanges." "Participants in the marketing exchange process should be able to expect that 1. Products and services offered are safe and fit for their intended uses; 2. Communications about offered products and services are not deceptive; 3. All parties intend to discharge their obligations, financial or otherwise, in good faith; and 4. Appropriate internal methods exist for equitable adjustment and/or redress of grievances concerning purchases."

Marketing: "In the area of product development and management: [1] disclosure of all substantial risks associated with product or service usage; [2] identification of any product component substitution that might materially change the product or impact on the buyer's purchase decision; [3] identification of extra cost-added features."

Marketing: "In the area of promotions: [1] avoidance of false and misleading advertising; [2] rejection of high-pressure manipulations, or misleading sales tactics; [3] avoidance of sales promotions that use deception or manipulation."

Marketing: "In the area of distribution: [1] not manipulating the availability of a product for the purpose of exploitation; [2] not using coercion in the marketing channel; [3] not exerting undue influence over the reseller's choice to handle a product."

Marketing: "In the area of pricing: [1] not engaging in price fixing; [2] not practicing predatory pricing; [3] disclosing the full price associated with any purchase."

From the corporate world:

ExxonMobil Corporation: "The Corporation's policy is to . . . furnish accurate and sufficient information about its products and services, including details of guarantees and warranties, so that customers can make informed purchasing decisions."

Wal-Mart: "As Wal-Mart Associates and Directors we must: . . . never manipulate, misrepresent, abuse or conceal information."

Wal-Mart: "Wal-Mart bases its relationships with suppliers on lawful, efficient and fair business practices. The selection of suppliers must be made on the basis of objective criteria, including quality, price, delivery, adherence to schedules, product suitability, maintenance of adequate sources of supply and Wal-Mart's purchasing practices and procedures."

Home Depot: "Each Director, Officer and Associate should always deal fairly with the Company's customers, suppliers, competitors and Associates. None should take unfair advantage of anyone through manipulation, concealment, abuse of privileged information, misrepresentation of material facts, or any other unfair practice."

Home Depot: "We will be professional and fair in all of our dealings with our vendors and suppliers. We will select business partners whose values and business practices are compatible with our own high standards so that we can build lasting relationships that enable us to grow and prosper in a competitive marketplace."

Citigroup Inc.: "Citigroup is committed to dealing fairly with its customers, suppliers, competitors and employees. No person may take unfair advantage of anyone through manipulation, concealment, abuse of confidential information, misrepresentation of material facts or other unfair dealing practice."

Citigroup Inc.: "Citigroup purchases all goods and services on the basis of price, quality, availability, terms and service. When Citigroup deals with other Citigroup businesses or customers, such transactions must be consistent with arm's length market terms and applicable law."

Boeing: "They observe that fair dealing is the foundation for all of our transactions and interactions."

The Kroger Co.: "Our customers have the right to adequate information concerning the prices of the items they purchase and the assurance that their purchase, combining price and quality, represents a fair value."

Berkshire Hathaway Inc.: "No Covered Party should take unfair advantage of anyone through manipulation, concealment, abuse of privileged information, misrepresentation of material facts, or any other unfair practice."

Code of Ethics Guidance Regarding Distributive Justice

From the professions:

Human Resource Management: "Encourage my employer to make the fair and equitable treatment of all employees a primary concern."

From the corporate world:

Wal-Mart: "Our Company is committed to maintaining an environment in which our Associates are proud to work, our suppliers and other business partners know that they are being dealt with fairly, and our shareholders can invest with confidence."

Wal-Mart: "Wal-Mart Associates should treat each other with dignity and respect. We should be fair and courteous in all of our interactions in the workplace."

Notes

1   George Long (trans.), *The Meditations of Marcus Aurelius* (New York: Avon Books, 1993), 48.

2   Adam Smith, *The Theory of Moral Sentiments* (Indianapolis: Liberty Fund, 1984), 175.

3   Daniel Kahneman, Jack L. Knetsch, and Richard Thaler, "Fairness as a Constraint on Profit Seeking: Entitlements in the Market," *American Economic Review* 76 (1986):728.

4   David Wood, "Business Justice: Transactions, Resources, and Organizations," *Journal of Business Ethics* 13 (1994): 482-483.

5   David M. Holley, "Information Disclosure in Sales," *Journal of Business Ethics* 17 (1998): 632.

6   Albert Z. Carr, "Is Business Bluffing Ethical?," *Harvard Business Review,* January-February 1968: 152.

7   Holley, "Information Disclosure in Sales," 632-633.

8   American Marketing Association, "Code of Ethics" http://www.3-media.com/ama.html.

9   Edward J. O'Boyle & Lyndon E. Dawson, "The American Marketing Association Code of Ethics: Instructions for Marketers," *Journal of Business Ethics* 11 (1992): 925-926.

10 Immanuel Kant, *Foundations of the Metaphysic of Morals,* 1785 (New York: Macmillian, 1990), 46.

11 Christine Korsgard, *Creating the Kingdom of Ends* (New York: Cambridge University Press, 1996), 167.

12 Tom Morris, *If Aristotle Ran General Motors* (New York: Henry Holt and Company, 1997), 188.

13 David Olive, *Just Rewards: The Case for Ethical Reform in Business* (Toronto: Key Porter Books, 1987), 56.

14 O'Boyle & Dawson, "The American Marketing Association Code," 926.

15 Samuel V. Bruton, "Teaching the Golden Rule," *Journal of Business Ethics* 49 (2004): 180.

16 Morris, *If Aristotle Ran General Motors,* 146-147.

17 Bruton, "Teaching the Golden Rule," 181.

18 Bruton, "Teaching the Golden Rule," 182.

19 Bruton, "Teaching the Golden Rule," 182.

20 Bruton, "Teaching the Golden Rule," 182-183.

21 Bruton, "Teaching the Golden Rule," 186.

22 Bruton, "Teaching the Golden Rule," 186.

23 Surendra Arjoon, "Virtue Theory as a Dynamic Theory of Business," *Journal of Business Ethics* 28 (2000): 159-178.

Text Box Footnotes

Plato, Laws, "There are not many..." David Olive, *Just Rewards: The Case for Ethical Reform in Business* (Toronto: Key Porter Books, 1987), 37.

John Lavater, "He who fairly praises..." Ted Goodman, ed., *The Forbes Book of Business Quotations* (New York: Black Dog & Leventhal Publishers, Inc., 1997), 409.

Plato, "Among the characteristics..." Thomas Cleary, trans., *Living a Good Life* (Boston: Shambhala, 1997), 50.

Aristotle, "Friendship among citizens..." As quoted in William J. Bennett, *Our Sacred Honor* (Nashville: Broadman & Holman Publishers, 1997), 147.

Ralph Waldo Emerson, "Every man takes care..." Ted Goodman, ed., *The Forbes Book of Business Quotations* (New York: Black Dog & Leventhal Publishers, Inc., 1997), 190.

Choose to Be Thorough and Critical in Decision-Making

" Too many businessmen never stop to ponder what they
   are doing; they reject the need for self-discipline; they
   are satisfied to be clever, when they need to be wise."[1]
   - Louis Finkelstein

The influential Stoic philosopher Marcus Aurelius, Roman Emperor from 161-180 A.D., paid tribute to a habit of mind he learned from his father, Annius Verus:

> In my father I observed . . . his habit of careful
> inquiry in all matters of deliberation, and his
> persistency, and that he never stopped his
> investigation through being satisfied with
> appearances which first present themselves;. . .

for he was a man who looked to what ought to be done, not to the reputation which is got by a man's acts. He examined all things severally as if he had abundance of time, and without confusion, in an orderly way, vigorously and consistently.[2]

In this brief description, Marcus Aurelius identifies the most important characteristics of ethical decision-making: consistently careful, persistent, deliberate critical thinking, uninfluenced by irrelevant outside influences. We can summarize by saying that an ethical thinker takes an approach to information and courses of action that is thorough and critical.

Rational human beings think before they act. The ability to act according to a sense of rightness, unimpaired by passions and drives, and to accurately predict the outcomes of actions, is a reflection of mental maturity. When people lack this ability, or simply neglect to act in accordance with it, they are controlled by instincts and external stimuli. They lack what Richard T. DeGeorge refers to as "the rational freedom of self-determination."[3]

> " I want employees to ask themselves whether they are willing to have any contemplated act appear the next day on the front page of their local paper – to be read by their spouses, children and friends – with the reporting done by an informed and critical reporter."
>
> – Warren Buffett

In many instances, codes of conduct are useful in guiding decisions. However, especially at levels of authority where tough decisions are made, decision-making requires more effort and more wisdom than will be found in any code. Deciding what is right requires an evaluation of the objectives of the act and a determination of whether ethical considerations affect the rightness of the decision. For example, what is right according to how it will affect share price may yield an entirely different decision than what is right according to what is ethically excellent.[4]

Being Thorough - Is it enough?

If we accept the notion that ethically excellent decision-makers are thorough, how thorough do they need to be? Is there a point of diminishing returns? Abraham Lincoln emphasized the need to "take time and think well upon [a] subject. Nothing valuable," he said "can be lost by taking time."[5] But how much time? When does taking more time become counter-productive?

One of the challenging and significant judgments that decision-makers are called upon to make, particularly in a professional setting, is deciding when they have done enough. Factors that can impact their determinations include time constraints, laziness, habit, and conventional practice. The examples that follow present dilemmas faced by professionals in which determinations must be made regarding the completeness of their work.

- Jane is a financial auditor. She has been assigned the responsibility to observe the counting of a client's inventories. At the end of the day, she compares her test count and inventory tag control sheets with the summaries that the company has prepared that will be used in the valuation of the inventories. In one particular area of the warehouse she finds significant discrepancies in a few of the counts. She confronts her client with the news of the discrepancies. The client explains that after she left that area, some of the inventory was repositioned. Jane now recognizes that she should have done a better job at controlling movements of the inventory. She is working on a tight budget and must decide whether additional procedures are necessary to satisfy her as to the accuracy of the inventory counts. She has participated in the audit for several years and believes she has every reason to trust her client. Should she demand a recount in the areas of discrepancy? If she does, it will clearly cause her to exceed the audit budget and will irritate the client.

- Max is an investment counselor. His clients are willing to accept Max's sometimes aggressive investment advice. In the past, Max's advice has allowed his clients to make profits in their investments that are far superior to those they made prior to meeting Max. Max receives a call from a friend who has become aware of an investment opportunity in a new company that is paying returns on investments at eight percent per month! Max's friend discloses that he has become aware of the opportunity through "a friend of a friend." Max knows nothing more about the opportunity, but the expected returns seem tremendous, and the time window of opportunity is narrow. Max's friend discloses that he knows the promised returns are real because he invested in this company himself and received the first two months of the promised return. Based on this information, should Max invest his clients' money in this investment?

- Carla is a high school advanced placement calculus teacher. The students she teaches are dependent on her to introduce them to the concepts necessary to be successful in their national exams. The students are complaining that they have absorbed as much calculus as they can handle. Carla reasons that these sixteen-, seventeen-, and eighteen-year-olds are mature enough to assume responsibility for their own learning, and it is high time they face the consequence of their resistance to learning. Should Carla relax the pace of learning?

The answers to the questions posed in each of these examples should seem obvious. Yet, in these examples, if Jane, Max, and Carla make the expedient decision, it will probably have a significant impact on others. The extra effort required will surely have its immediate cost. Nevertheless, each has to evaluate whether the effort is sufficient.

Being Critical - Is it right?

I have asserted that ethical decision-makers should be critical in their analysis. The choice of the word critical needs some explanation. Critical thinking, in this sense, is thinking that is careful, evaluative, and sometimes skeptical. Critical thinking is involved in making the difficult decisions that many find too challenging to make. Critical thinking might involve asking difficult questions such as:

- Do I continue to do business with him after he withheld an essential fact from me on the last occasion I dealt with him?

- Does associating with him in a joint effort affect my reputation in such a way that it would be improper for me to continue?

- Is it time to terminate his employment with the company?

- How do I deal with pressures to improve reported results when the actual results are not that good?

The need for critical thinking is based in part on the recognition that not all decisions are routine and ethically clear. While an organization's code of conduct and its standard practices may provide a conclusive basis for making a routine decision, it may be only a useful tool when the more challenging decisions are made. Prior personal experiences, a sense of what constitutes correct principles, and the wisdom of others will likely need to be considered in making these tough decisions.

" What has not been examined impartially has not been well examined. Skepticism is therefore the first step toward truth."– Denis Diderot

As with the obligation to be thorough, there are admittedly time constraints associated with critical thinking. Decision-makers cannot be skeptical all of the time, and the process of evaluation in any situation eventually must end. Experience and alertness, therefore,

> *"* **Every great mistake has a halfway moment, a split second when it can be recalled and perhaps remedied."**
>
> *– Pearl S. Buck*

are important in deciding when the situation warrants continued evaluation and taking shorter steps forward, and when it is time to make a final judgment about intended actions. Slowing down long enough to make correct decisions is often the proper course. But knowing when to move boldly forward is required of strong leaders.

Compassion and Risk

Experience tells us all that we cannot expect everyone with whom we do business to operate according to conventional moral standards. A sense of compassion arising from our own moral inclinations might influence how we deal with such people. We may be inclined to forgive when we have been wronged, and to take the risk of giving others a second chance. Even as we do this, we should be wary, as the wisest of advisors would counsel us: Jesus taught his disciples to be "wise as serpents, and harmless as doves."[6] Aristotle advised, "Decency is not cheating anyone, and intelligence is not being cheated by anyone."[7] William Shakespeare warned, "Love all, trust a few. Do wrong to none."[8] And Abraham Lincoln cautioned, "Stand with anybody that stands right . . . and part with him when he goes wrong."[9] While I have emphasized that ethically excellent behavior sometimes requires sacrifice, it does not require accepting the role of victim to the actions of the cheater.

Groupthink

In the workplace, premiums are often placed on characteristics such as loyalty, cooperation, unanimity, and respect for authority. On the face of things, it would seem that such characteristics would make for a particularly effective workplace. But loyalty, cooperation, consensus, and respect for authority can all be misplaced virtues under certain circumstances and, when unchecked, can lead to a condition known as *groupthink*.

Groupthink can arise among people who have common goals when members of the group begin to choose to refrain from independently evaluating and questioning the correctness of decisions being made within the group. The silence of individual group members often arises from a desire to avoid conflict and thereby to appear to be team players. The culture of the organization and the unreflecting habits of its members begin to dominate the decisions made by the group. A commitment to individual ethical standards, even at conventional levels, is sometimes absent as collective arrogance and pride become the dominant characteristics of the group.

Those in the snare of groupthink may find it easy to rationalize incorrect decisions because the motivations for going along with the group may seem virtuous (showing respect for the opinions of others is a good thing to do) or may seem to be justifiable by virtuous ends (it doesn't matter what we do along the way, because the reason we're doing it is to maximize profits for our organization). It is frequently the case that when profits are the only virtuous ends, groupthink "justifies" cheating to get advantage over others in order to achieve ends that are not otherwise achievable. These artificial achievements are touted as "evidence" of the correctness of the group thought. In fact, they are nothing more than rationalizations designed to avoid responsibility for wrong thinking.

Though groupthink can result in rapid, unanimous decisions, it should not be mistaken for true decisiveness. Groupthink has little patience for careful consideration of all relevant facts and pertinent alternative solutions. Moreover, when groupthink becomes the culture of a group or organization, the awareness and sensitivities of its members can be affected.

> " We will walk on our own feet; we will work with our own hands; we will speak our own minds."
>
> – Ralph Waldo Emerson

Those engaged in groupthink are less inclined to independent thinking and can become less alert to danger signals and less sensitive to violations of their own ethical standards. In fact, a groupthink culture discourages the airing of concerns associated with ethical issues and may create a need to ignore warnings and to spin interpretations of events and information, so that dissenting opinions do not merely present alternatives; they must be seen as wrong.

Dissenting opinions associated with ethical matters can be delicate, as determinations of what is right and what is wrong are often the subject of personal beliefs. Respecting dissent within an organization and giving it time to produce useful results can be difficult. But allowing time for consideration of alternative points of view and creative thinking processes is not only ethically proper; wise leaders know that it can give a competitive edge in a difficult market.

Groupthink often develops within organizations whose leaders are particularly autocratic. Contrary to Kant's assertion that all others must be treated as ends in themselves, autocratic leaders treat their employees functionally, expecting them to meet established objectives of efficiency and productivity and to ignore individual thinking.[10] Subordinates in such a situation fear the consequences of offering dissenting opinions, and few opportunities exist for reconsideration of decisions made "from on high." Because those who are new to the work environment tend to accept the culture of the organization, they are not likely to try to impose their sense of ethical behavior on the organization when they find it contrary to what they have learned at home and in school. They are more likely to move along with what William Wordsworth referred to as "the unreflecting herd."[11]

"When all think alike, then no one is thinking."

— Walter Lippmann

Groupthink can have as a consequence an undue focus on objectives that are universally common, excluding other objectives particular to the organization. For example, the objective of short-term profits is often universally acceptable to a profit-making enterprise. If the group seeking unanimity can easily settle on that objective alone, their tendency may be to avoid worthwhile, alternative objectives. So powerful can the groupthink influence be that ordinary people whose inclinations are to be ethical can be persuaded to engage in activities that are clearly unethical. For example, several years ago Equity Funding established their "Department 99," into which were assigned non-existent insurance policies that were created by the employees, many of them new to the organization. Department 99 held "manufacturing parties" where the fictitious insurance policies were created. It "became a joke, a game. People laughed and laughed about it."[12]

The ethical behaviors of top management personnel have the greatest impact on the culture of an organization. In some of the most famous business frauds, top management lacked ethical commitment. When this occurs, the written codes of conduct become meaningless, and efforts of lower-level leaders to have a positive ethical influence on those working under their direction will have little impact on the behavior of the organization.

Any work-related organization wishing to avoid serious mistakes must be willing to provide an orderly means for members to critically consider and report their independent determinations in a non-threatening way. Committees charged with making important decisions should establish a devil's-advocate methodology so that alternative solutions can be zealously presented. This is most effective when the assignment of arguing

> **"There are always two choices, two paths to take. One is easy, and that is its only reward."**
>
> *– Unknown*

an opposing point of view is rotated among the members, so that no one person earns a false reputation for rebelliousness.[13]

Steps to Making Important Decisions

Many ordinary decisions, because of their lack of complexity, can be made without much deliberation. Rules, routines, and prior deliberations allow for quick decision-making. Often, however, especially at management levels, decisions made without careful deliberation can mean trouble. Since the success, even the continued existence, of the organization, not to mention the happiness and well-being of the organization's members, can depend on such decisions being right,[14] organizations may retain and promote people based on their abilities to make difficult decisions.

How does a person make the important decisions? Here are some suggested steps:[15]

1   Be alert to the fact that dilemmas may exist.

2.   Gather all the facts. Write them down.

3.   Identify possible solutions. Write them down.

4.   Evaluate possible solutions in terms of principles, rules, consequences, and sense of rightness, conferring with others as appropriate.

5.   Make the decision. Write it down, along with the basis for the conclusion.

6.   *When appropriate*, notify others - including superiors, favorite advisors, and persons impacted by the decision - ahead of the action.

7.   Act!

Step 1: Be alert to the fact that dilemmas may exist.

It is especially difficult to anticipate problems when the normal course of activities does not suggest impending danger.

Business is a dynamic environment in which change and problems often come unexpectedly.[16] We may turn again to the words of Marcus Aurelius for a warning:

> Just in the same way ought we to act all through
> life, and where there are things which appear most
> worthy of our approbation, we ought to lay them
> bare and look at their worthlessness, and strip
> them of all the words by which they are exalted.
> For outward show is a wonderful perverter of the
> reason, and when thou are most sure that thou are
> employed about things worth thy pains, it is then
> that it cheats thee most.[17]

A business acquaintance of mine went to work as an internal accountant for a company now known for fraudulent activities that eventually led to its spectacular failure. My friend is a CPA and, based on my interactions with him, I can affirm that he is reasonably bright. He was in a position to work daily with the books and records of the company and to evaluate their credibility. It was later learned that the vast majority of the company's revenues and profits were completely fictitious. My acquaintance did not become aware of the existence of the fraud until after it was disclosed by someone outside the company. It is difficult to understand how fraud of this magnitude could have been missed by the company insiders, except to speculate that many of those within the company were asleep on the job.

English poet, painter, and engraver William Blake offered some practical advice regarding how people can bring some order to their daily activities so that they might be more effective: "Think in the morning. Act in the noon. Eat in the evening. Sleep in the night."[18] Unfortunately, too many of us tend to neglect the "think in the morning" part.

Those who participate in an organization's activities only part-time, such as members of boards of directors, can be especially vulnerable to surprise. The financial difficulties suffered during the final years of Sir Walter Scott's life are on point. Scott served as a director of the Edinburgh Assurance Company during the early 1800s, the days before directors' and officers' insurance provided some protection to the members of the board. Scott attended yearly meetings of the company. An entry in his diary in 1825 suggests the casual manner in which he approached his role on the board: "Went to the yearly court of the Edinburgh Assurance Co. to which I am one of those graceful useless appendages called 'Directors Extraordinary.'" During that same year, Scott was shocked to discover that with the failure of the publishing house of Hurst & Robinson, Scott was held personally liable on debts totaling £130,000. He spent the last seven years of his life attempting to pay off this debt by writing. He is said to have died of exhaustion.

Step 2: Gather all the facts. Write them down.

Critical thinking involves patiently observing, gathering facts, and then reflecting upon what has been discovered. As the facts are gathered they are related to the known information, and they serve as a basis for challenging the accuracy of what was previously understood. First

> **"It is a capital mistake to theorize before one has data."**
> – Arthur Conan Doyle

impressions can yield the easy solutions, but these are not necessarily the best solutions. Too often, the tendency is to gather just enough information to justify a hasty decision, rather than to continue to gather facts sufficient to make a better one.

Many people resist the process of gathering details, as they see themselves at a level of importance that is above the space where the "small stuff" seems to exist. Such an attitude frequently proves to be a big mistake, since when the light of day shines on a bad decision,

> **"The man who is at the top is a man who has the habit of getting to the bottom."**
> – Joseph E. Rogers

the failure to find available information, at whatever level, becomes suddenly transferable to the person who made the decision.

Taking time to write ideas or concerns out is a useful tool for clarifying thinking when dealing with challenging situations. Writing thoughts down suggests particular concern for the issue at hand. It allows the information to be viewed more objectively. Imagining that someone else is going to read it later encourages more careful and rational thinking, assuming, of course, that great care is taken in the process to present the best thinking.

Step 3: Identify possible solutions. Write them down.

In identifying possible solutions, keeping the mind open to alternative resolutions is essential. This involves creative thinking, even thinking that may not be consistent with a sense of what is right.

Let me cite a personal example regarding the importance of this step. In my work as a fraud investigator, I have learned that

I am most successful in discovering the evidence of wrongdoing when I remember to "think like a thief." In other words, I have to place myself in the shoes of the person who has an opportunity to carry out the fraudulent act and decide how someone in that state of mind would act. I cannot limit my thinking to what someone else thinks has happened or to what my past experience suggests might have occurred. Identifying all of the possible ways in which fraud might occur allows me to be more thorough and, therefore, more successful.

Again, writing the alternative solutions down allows us to organize our thoughts. It is part of the discovery process and often leads to a need to revisit Step 2.

Step 4: Evaluate possible solutions in terms of principles, rules, consequences, and sense of rightness, conferring with others as appropriate.

The gathered facts are best observed in relationship to one another and then in relationship to principles and ideals. Testing the options involves determining whether something is right based on a decision-making model. If we are inclined to a deontological model, where we emphasize following the rules and expecting them to yield positive consequences, then we will be more apt to evaluate the options based on our perception

> "Sunlight is the most powerful of all disinfectants."
>
> – Louis D. Brandeis
> U.S. Supreme Court Justice

of the applicable rules. On the other hand, if our orientation is more towards utilitarianism, believing that what is most moral is that which produces the best results for all people involved, we will be more apt to evaluate the consequences of the action. A truly thorough evaluation would consider both approaches.

When dilemmas arise in any environment, ethical solutions should be the goal. Ethical analysis can involve various models[19] or maxims:

- The *Golden Rule*. This approach asks people to consider how they would want to be treated.

- A *utilitarian model*. This approach attempts to measure the happiness and misery that alternative solutions will provide and seeks the solution that maximizes the happiness and minimizes the misery.

- A *professional ethic model*. The guidelines of a profession determine that a correct approach would be based on how other independent professionals would view an action.

- *Enlightened-egoist model*. This approach allows persons to act in their own self-interest, as long as others are not hurt by the actions.

- *Kant's formulaions of the Categorical Imperative*. Decision-makers determine whether it is logical to conclude that if something is right for them, it must be right for all other rational human beings.

- *Light-of-day model*. When attempting to determine the rightness of a matter, decision-makers attempt to determine how the action will appear at a later time, when the "light of day" shines on all of the facts and circumstances.

We can easily predict that as reasonable people employ alternative models to solve ethical dilemmas, differing, even conflicting, solutions may appear for a single problem. This highlights an important truth: not all ethical dilemmas have one and only one agreeable solution.

Conferring with others thus becomes an important form of testing for the best solution, both as to the rightness of the decision, and as to the expected resolve to carry it out. The best critical thinking involves asking questions and listening to others. Management guru Peter Drucker reflects that his "greatest strength as a consultant is to be ignorant and ask a few questions."[20]

Of course, ultimately, decision-makers should be expected to make their own decisions. But, especially at times when emotions are likely to affect judgment, or when additional facts would shed light or create possibilities, or when more wisdom could broaden perspective, considering the advice of others can be invaluable. Discussion with others allows discovery and understanding of alternative interpretations of the facts. It allows testing

" He that is taught only by himself has a fool for a master." – Ben Johnson

of assessments of principles, rules, and consequences against someone else's interpretations, and discovery of whether these assessments can be supported by appropriate reasoning. As British economist John Maynard Keynes, father of modern macroeconomics, once observed, "It is astonishing what foolish things one can temporarily believe if one thinks too long alone."[21]

Step 5: Make the decision. Write it down, along with the basis for the conclusion.

Having identified and tested the options, the next step is to make the decision. If the investigation of the facts is complete and the options have been tested, chances are more likely that the decision will be clear and correct.

Writing down the basis for the conclusion is a critical step in the evaluation process. The goal should be that the basis for the decision be persuasive.

" No trumpets sound when the important decisions of our life are made. Destiny is made known silently."

– Agnes DeMille

Step 6: When appropriate, notify others - including superiors, favorite advisors, and persons impacted by the decision - ahead of the action.

Occasionally, especially when a face-to-face confrontation has the potential to generate anger and resentment, I write comments in the form of a memo or a letter. And then I work to have the self-control not to send the letter. In this practice I follow the advice of Abraham Lincoln: "Write letters of refutation that vent your anger and emotions, but do not mail them." Another U.S. president, Harry S Truman, on one occasion got the first part of Lincoln's advice right, but regrettably failed on the second. Margaret Truman, the President's daughter, sang before 3,500 people at Constitution Hall in Washington, D.C. On the

next morning, President Truman opened the *Washington Post* and
read a review by music critic Paul Hume:

> Miss Truman is a unique American phenomenon
> with a pleasant voice of little size and fair quality.
> She is extremely attractive on stage.
>
> . . . Yet Miss Truman cannot sing very well. She is
> flat a good deal of the time - more last night than
> at any time we have heard her in past years. There
> are few moments during her recital when one can
> relax and feel confident that she will make her
> goal, which is the end of the song.
>
> Miss Truman has not improved in the years we
> have heard her . . . she still cannot sing with
> anything approaching professional finish.
>
> She communicates almost nothing of the music
> she presents . . . And still the public goes and pays
> the same price it would for the world's finest
> singers . . . .
>
> It is an extremely unpleasant duty to record such
> unhappy facts about so honestly appealing a
> person. But as long as Miss Truman sings as she
> has for three years, and does today, we seem to
> have no recourse unless it is to omit comment on
> her programs altogether.[22]

The day before, President Truman's press advisor and closest confidant, Charlie Ross, had suddenly passed away from a heart attack. The President was naturally under stress over the loss of his friend when he opened his copy of the *Washington Post* at 5:30 a.m. the next day. When he read Hume's review, he snapped. President Truman was so angry that he pulled out a White House memo pad and wrote a scathing reply to Mr. Hume's review. He sealed it up, affixed a three-cent stamp to the envelope, and personally dropped it off in a mailbox on the street. The contents of the letter eventually ended up on the front page of the *Washington News*. It read:

> Mr Hume: I've just read your lousy review of Margaret's concert. I've come to the conclusion that you are an "eight ulcer man on four ulcer pay."

> It seems to me that you are a frustrated old man [Hume was thirty-four] who wishes he could have been successful. When you write such poppy-cock as was in the back section of the paper you work for, it shows conclusively that you're off the beam and at least four of your ulcers are at work.

> Some day I hope to meet you. When that happens you'll need a new nose, a lot of beefsteak for black eyes, . . . !

> [Westbrook] Pegler, a gutter snipe, is a gentleman alongside you. I hope you'll accept that statement as a worse insult than a reflection on your ancestry.[23]

Unfortunately for the President, his trusted confidant was not available to advise him as to the propriety of sending such a letter. When confronted with the news of her father's reply to Hume, the President's daughter refused to believe it, saying that he did not have time to write such a letter and would not use that kind of language. President Truman privately admitted that he should never have written the letter.[24] Had Charlie Ross been available for consultation, the President's angry letter no doubt would never have been sent. A lesson for us all.

Step 7: Act.

"Failures are divided into two classes - those who thought and never did, and those who did and never thought."[25] Acting according to our convictions can be a significant challenge. But having given adequate attention to the investigative process described above, it is time to proceed with determination.

It is important to recognize that as decision-makers go through this seven-step process, the results of any one of the steps may create a need to return to an earlier step. Conferring with others, for example, may result in the need to gather additional facts or to consider another possible solution. The mindset of being thorough and critical requires this sometimes lengthy process, and a strong sense of integrity should demand this level of effort.

Being thorough and critical implies having the ability to give proper weight to values and to sort out the extreme applications of those values, especially loyalty, duty, dedication, and sacrifice. It implies being able to recognize rationalization without being overwhelmed by its apparent logic and convenience. It involves gathering sufficient facts so that impressions become understandings. It implies being alert and having the courage to object when appropriate. In short, being thorough and critical is about being patient, about developing a clearer picture of the expected end, and about being willing to sometimes take the more difficult path.

" **And if thou seest clear, go by this way content, without turning back: but if thou dost not see clear, stop and take the best advisers. But if any other things oppose thee, go on according to thy powers with due consideration, keeping to that which appears to be just.**"

– *Marcus Aurelius*

Code of Ethics Guidance Regarding Decision-Making

From the professions:

Accounting: Article I: Accountants "exercise sensitive professional and moral judgments in all their activities." Article IV "avoid any subordination of their judgment."

Education: Principle II (Commitment to the Profession) Educators "shall exert every effort to promote a climate that encourages the exercise of professional judgment."

Law: Cannon 5: "A lawyer should exercise independent professional judgment on behalf of a client."

Marketing: "Marketers must accept responsibility for the consequences of their activities and make every effort to ensure that their decisions, recommendations and actions function to identify, serve and satisfy all relevant publics: customers, organizations and society."

Medical: Principle V: Physicians "make relevant information available to patients, colleagues, and the public, obtain consultation, and use the talents of other health professionals when indicated."

From the corporate world:

ExxonMobil Corporation: "While we maintain flexibility to adapt to changing conditions, the nature of our business requires a focused, long term approach."

Wal-Mart: "It is also our responsibility to apply common sense, together with a desire simply to do the right thing, in making business and personal decisions where no stated guideline exists."

Wal-Mart: "In the final analysis, you must rely on your own good judgment and sense of ethical behavior to make sure that you are always doing the right thing."

Citigroup Inc.: "You should use your judgment and common sense; if something seems unethical or improper, it probably is."

Citigroup Inc.: "Citigroup has established business practices committees, at the corporate level and in each of its business units, which work to ensure that our most senior executives regularly scrutinize our practices and products, and potential conflicts of interest; that our policies are appropriate; and that our basic values are emphasized at every level throughout the organization. The business unit committees identify business practices that may raise these concerns, subject them to rigorous scrutiny and present them to senior executives to decide whether changes are required."

Citigroup Inc.: "You must use common sense and observe standards of good taste regarding content and language when creating business records and other documents (such as e-mail) that may be retained by Citigroup or a third party. You should keep in mind that at a future date, Citigroup or a third party may be in a position to rely on or interpret the document with the benefit of hindsight and/or the disadvantage of imperfect recollections."

Citigroup Inc.: "Citigroup necessarily relies on your commitment to exercise sound judgment, to seek advice when appropriate . . . ."

The Kroger Co.: "All such acts should be undertaken with the expectation that they will become publicly known."

The Kroger Co.: "We are expected to exercise good judgment as well as moral courage in matters of investigation and reporting covered by this document."

Notes

1   Louis Finkelstein, "The Businessman's Moral Failure," *Fortune*, September 1958: 116.

2   George Long (trans.), *The Meditations of Marcus Aurelius* (New York: Avon Books, 1993), 7.

3   Richard T. DeGeorge, *Business Ethics, Fourth Edition* (New Jersey: Prentice Hall, 1995), 91-92.

4   Pietra Rivoli, "Ethical Aspects of Investor Behavior," *Journal of Business Ethics* 14 (1995): 266.

5   As quoted in Donald T. Phillips, *Lincoln on Leadership* (New York: Warner Books, 1992), 76.

6   St. Matthew 10:16.

7   Thomas Cleary (trans.), *Living the Good Life* (Boston: Shambhala, 1997), 65.

8   William Shakespeare, *All's Well That Ends Well,* act 1, sc. 1, 1. 64-5. As quoted in http://www.bartleby.com/66/50/50750.html.

9   Abraham Lincoln, *Collected Works of Abraham Lincoln* (Peoria, Illinois: Rutgers University Press, 1953, 1990), vol 2, p. 273. As quoted in http://www.bartleby.com/66/78/36278.html.

10 Oliver F. Williams and John W. Houck (eds.), *A Virtuous Life in Business* (Lanham, Maryland: Rowman & Littlefield Publishers, Inc., 1992), 17.

11 William Wordsworth, *The Complete Poetical Works* (London: Macmillan and Co., 1888). As quoted in http://www.bartleby.com/br/145.html.

12 William E. Blundel, "Some Assets Missing, Insurance Called Bogus at Equity Funding Life," *Wall Street Journal*, April 2, 1973: 1.

13 R. A. Cosier and C.R. Schwenk, "Agreement and Thinking Alike: Ingredients for Poor Decisions," *Academy of Management Executive* 4: 69-74 as quoted in Ronald R. Sims, "Linking Groupthink to Unethical Behavior in Organizations," *Journal of Business Ethics* 11 (1992): 659.

14 Ronald R. Sims, "The Challenge of Ethical Behavior in Organizations," *Journal of Business Ethics,* 11 (1992): 512.

15 J.R. Schermerhorn, *Management for Productivity* (New York: John Wiley, 1989) and A.L. Otten, "Ethics on the Job: Companies Alert Employees to Potential Dilemmas," *The Wall Street Journal,* July 14, 1986: 17, as referenced in Sims, "The Challenge of Ethical Behavior," 512.

16 Sims, "The Challenge of Ethical Behavior," 505.

17 Long, trans., *The Meditations of Marcus Aurelius*, 41.

18 As quoted in http://www.memorablequotations.com.

19 Robert Allan Cooke, "Danger Signs of Unethical Behavior: How to Determine If Your Firm Is at Ethical Risk," *Journal of Business Ethics* 10 (1991): 251. Also, Gene R. Laczniak and Patrick E. Murphy, "Fostering Ethical Marketing Decisions," *Journal of Business Ethics,* 10 (1991): 264.

20 As quoted in "Thought-of-the-Day Archive," http://www.refdesk.com, August 2, 2004.

21 As quoted in http://www.executive-forum.com.

22 David McCullough, *Truman* (New York: Simon & Schuster, 1992), 827-828.

23 McCullough, *Truman*, 829.

24 McCullough, *Truman*, 829.

25 Attributed to John Charles Salak, as quoted in http://www.motivatingquotes.com/failure.htm.

Text Box Footnotes

Warren Buffett, "I want employees..." CTB,Inc.,http://www.ctbinc.com/PDFfiles/Bershire %20 Code %20 of %20 Business %20 Conduct.pdf.

Denis Diderot, "What has not been examined..." Ted Goodman, ed., *The Forbes Book of Business Quotations* (New York: Black Dog & Leventhal Publishers, Inc., 1997), 852.

Pearl S. Buck, "Every great mistake..."Bartelby.com, http://www.bartleby.com.

Ralph Waldo Emerson, "We will walk on..." America Online and Bartleby.com, http://www.aol.bartleby.com/5/101.html.

Walter Lippman, "When we all think alike..." As quoted in Tom Morris, *If Aristotle Ran General Motors* (New York: Henry Holt and Company, 1997), 61.

Unknown, "There are always two choices..." Boise State University, http://www.boisestate.edu/staff/leadership/leadershipdef.htm.

Arthur Conan Doyle, "It is a capital mistake to theorize..." Robert Andrews, Mary Biggs, Michael Seidel, et al, eds., *The Columbia World of Quotations* (New York: Columbia University Press, 1996).

Joseph E. Rogers, "The man who is at the top..." Ted Goodman, ed., *The Forbes Book of Business Quotations* (New York: Black Dog & Leventhal Publishers, Inc., 1997), 117.

Louis D. Brandeis, "Sunlight is the most powerful..." Cornell University, http://www.supct.law.cornell.edu/supct/html/historics/US.

Ben Johnson, "He that is taught..." World of Quotes.com, http://www.worldofquotes.com/topic/Advice-Experience- Wisdom/9/.

Agnes DeMille, "No trumpets sound..." Robert Andrews, Mary Biggs, and Michael Seidel, eds., *The Columbia World of Quotations* (New York: Columbia University Press, 1996). Http//www.worldofquotes.com/ topic/ Destiny/1/.

Marcus Aurelius, "And if thou seest clear..." George Long, trans., *The Meditations of Marcus Aurelius* (New York: Avon Books, 1993), 81.

Choice 6

Choose to Follow Through with Ethical Resolutions

" I love the man that can smile in trouble, that can gather strength from distress, and grow brave by reflection. 'Tis the business of little minds to shrink; but he whose heart is firm, and whose conscience approves his conduct, will pursue his principles unto death."[1] - *Thomas Paine*

Everyone who has tried it knows that serious self-improvement is a difficult task. In his autobiographical *Plan for Moral Perfection*, Benjamin Franklin describes his efforts to perfect his character, in this instance his struggle to become more orderly and usefully methodical in the details of his life:

Order, too, with regard to places for things, papers, etc., I found extremely difficult to acquire. I had not been early accustomed to it, and, having an exceeding good memory, I was not so sensible of the inconvenience attending want of method. This article, therefore, cost me so much painful attention, and my faults in it vexed me so much, and I made so little progress in amendment, and had such frequent relapses, that I was almost ready to give up the attempt, and content myself with a faulty character in that respect, like the man who, in buying an ax of a smith, my neighbor, desired to have the whole of its surface as bright as the edge. The smith consented to grind it bright for him if he would turn the wheel; he turned, while the smith pressed the broad face of the ax hard and heavily on the stone, which made the turning of it very fatiguing. The man came every now and then from the wheel to see how the work went on, and at length would take his ax as it was, without farther grinding. "No," said the smith, "turn on, turn on; we shall have it bright by and by; as yet, it is only speckled." "Yes," says the man, "but I think I like a speckled ax best."[2]

Commitment to Follow Through

When we prepare to follow through with our ethical resolutions, we must recognize that some promises will be more difficult to keep than we anticipated when we made them and that it takes courage to do what is right when we are fortunate enough to know what is right. The common reaction when the task of completing commitments seems to grow harder is to settle for the speckled ax, complaining, "That's not what I had in mind when I entered into the agreement." The hard truth to face in such a situation is that if we had been more competent and diligent and more thorough and critical in the decision-making analysis, the dilemma might have been avoided. Nevertheless, unless we were defrauded in the process, our ethical obligation is to follow through with our commitment.

> **" Let honor be to us as strong an obligation as necessity is to others."** *–Pliny*

Organizational Contributions to an Ethical Environment

Senior management has a powerful influence on the behavior of others in the organization. They can establish an ethical culture by making ethical decisions on behalf of the organization. A classic example of the effect of top management decisions on the ethical culture of an organization is seen in Johnson & Johnson's handling of the situation that occurred when poison was added to a limited number of packages of their Tylenol product. They pulled all of their product from the marketplace. It cost them millions of dollars. But Johnson & Johnson's culture is to do what is right without regard to the cost. Imagine the effect on the Johnson & Johnson employees. Management made a decision that demonstrated, regardless of the cost, a real commitment to ethical behavior. Ethical actions contrary to that standard would have seemed out of place at Johnson & Johnson.

One of the most important practices an organization can put into place to encourage an ethical environment is not to punish dissenting points of view as long as the viewpoints are reasonable and consistent with the organization's proper objectives. As described in the previous chapter, organizations who attempt to eliminate groupthink conditions are more likely to arrive at ethically correct decisions. An environment where the expression of differing opinions is encouraged is one where the solutions to problems are not likely to be commenced with a whistleblower's complaint.

Ethical Conduct and Etiquette

Those who attempt to clearly define ethical behavior are sometimes challenged to distinguish between ethical behavior and etiquette.[3] While this distinction may be important to understanding the scope of ethical behavior, perhaps of more importance is understanding how ethics and etiquette might be related. A significant step a person can take in preparing to make ethical decisions is to develop habits that exhibit sensitivity, propriety, and kindness in relationships with others. Among these good habits are politeness, conscious awareness of the needs and interests of others, and the practice of keeping others properly informed. It is logical that if a person exhibits these characteristics in daily interactions, he will be more likely to act in an ethical manner when faced with difficult challenges.[4]

Establishing Ethical Standards

We all have moments when we wish we had made different decisions, when we wonder how things might have been better if we had done something differently. Perhaps we wish we could change something about our job or change the atmosphere within our home. Fortunately, there may be a way out of this all-too-common state.

It may seem ironic to some that the way out, the way to improve the atmosphere around us,

> " **Being faithful to a set of beliefs is more important than being successful.**"
>
> – Max De Pree

or to rectify the unpleasant results of past choices is to look inward—to improve ourselves, and to cease to settle for the speckled ax, as it were, and submit ourselves to some rigorous polishing. By setting standards of excellence for ourselves, we may find that it is not too late to make changes that will affect our attitudes, our happiness, and the way others behave around us. An important part of this process is to define what would constitute an atmosphere of integrity and goodness. Then we must be willing to live as if these conditions are the norms.

Many are reluctant to take such a course of action. Why is this? Are we afraid of the reactions of others if our personal ethical behavior seems strange to them?

Some years ago, while serving as a trustee in a large bankruptcy proceeding, I presided over a series of meetings associated with the sale of a shopping center to an entity from New York City. The representative of

> " **The choice is ours to make: to succeed at whatever the price or to accept the cost of being virtuous based on religious roots.**"
>
> – Oliver F. Williams & John W. Houch

the potential buyer was Jewish. As we were attempting to schedule our next meeting, he mentioned that our meeting would have to conclude by a certain time, allowing him to be home by sundown on Friday, since he and his family were observers of the Jewish Sabbath. He demonstrated no embarrassment over his request. I remember that my reaction was complete respect for this man's commitment, and I felt an absolute willingness to accommodate his needs. In my experience, most people, if they stop to think about it at all, wish they were living a more ethical existence, and they feel respect for those who demonstrate a strong commitment to do so.

Pressures, Opportunities, and Rationalizations

Figure 4

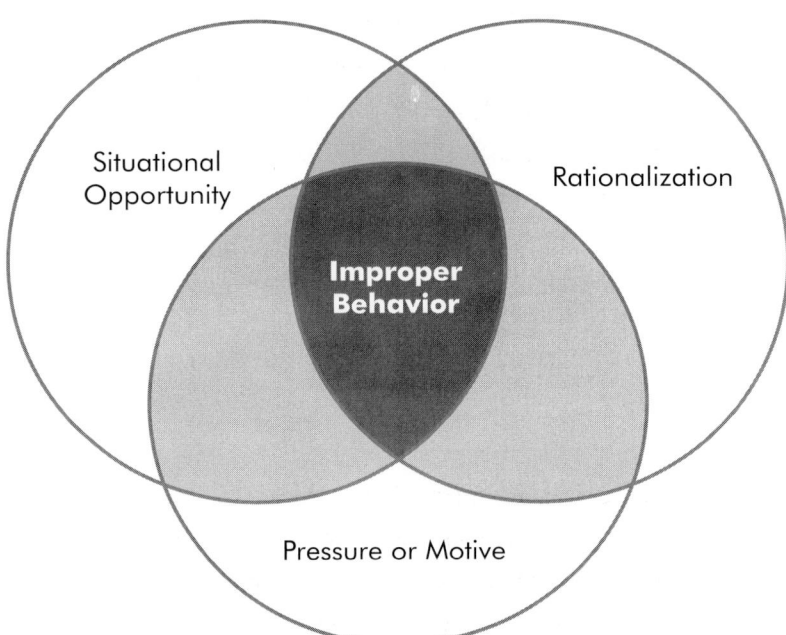

One of the important preparations a person can make to guard against unethical behavior is to become aware of the factors that converge to cause someone to depart from ethical behavior. There are three factors: a pressure, an opportunity, and a rationalization.

To illustrate, we can consider the example of Betty, the bookkeeper, who steals from her employer.

> Betty has been employed by ABC Bakery for twenty years. ABC bakes various bread products that are mostly distributed to grocery stores throughout the city. Additionally, the bakery has a counter where it sells its products to the public. Betty's husband has lost his job. Because they live from paycheck to paycheck and have a mortgage, a couple of car payments, and two children in college, Betty's family has depended heavily on her and her husband's paychecks. Betty is experiencing a *pressure* associated with a need for extra money for her family.
>
> Because of her faithful and trustworthy service to the company, the owner has not seen the need to establish accounting controls. One of Betty's responsibilities at the bakery is to deposit the currency and checks from sales at the front counter. Since the clerk does not use a cash register, no record is made of actual sales to reconcile with the collections. Betty merely picks up the receipts for the day, counts and records them, then deposits the coins, currency, and checks at the bank. Betty

has an *opportunity* to satisfy her need for extra
money.

Betty has worked hard for her employer. At various
times, especially with the month-end and the
year-end closings, she has worked long hours, and
because she is a salaried employee, she has not
been compensated for her extra effort. Over the
years the company has been successful in making a
lot of money for the owner. He certainly would not
miss the $1,000 cash she could easily take over the
course of a month. Betty has managed to come up
with a *rationalization* for taking the money.

What could Betty have done to avoid this unethical behavior?
First, she and her husband could have established a lifestyle
that allowed them to be less dependent on the two paychecks
coming every month, thereby lessening the *pressure* to take the
illicit funds. Second, as a bookkeeper, Betty should have felt
the need to establish accounting controls that would lessen
the *opportunity* for Betty or anyone else in the company to steal.
Third, Betty could have resolved to keep her commitments
to live with integrity and to avoid the *rationalizations* that lead
people to act unethically. It is important to observe that absent
any one of these factors the unethical behavior could not have
occurred.

Life offers unlimited combinations of pressures, opportunities,
and rationalizations that lead to unethical behavior. The ethical
person can prepare to avoid these unethical behaviors by
controlling or eliminating one or more of the three factors.

Pressures

The pressure Betty faced was not from her employer. Often, however, such pressure originates from within the company. Having experienced these types of pressures many times in my own work life and having investigated many others who have faced such challenges, my expectation is that nearly everyone who spends any substantial time in the workplace will be faced with unethical, even illegal, pressures generated from within their employment. Superiors often create pressures for employees to engage in illegal acts.

Many of the pressures in a corporate environment originate from expectations of the stakeholders of the company: investors, lenders, and managers. These pressures typically address the need to create earnings beyond the fair measures of actual activity. Sales are pre-booked, inventories are overstated, and measures of reserves are understated. Each of these activities is designed to enable reporting of income beyond its reality, and quite often these efforts require the assistance of many people. Unfortunately, those placed in the position to participate in such behavior do so for the sake of maintaining their jobs.

Beyond the business environment, pressures exist in all other forms of employment. Consider education, for example. Federal standards of student achievement require schools to demonstrate their effectiveness in educating youth. Students are prepared for the testing, and test results are reported. School administrators are pressured to show progress in relation to the federal standards and in relation to other schools. Students, likewise, feel pressures to succeed academically and in their extracurricular activities. Athletic programs are expected to demonstrate success on the playing field. Coaches may feel pressure to engage in improper recruiting activities, to falsify academic performance, to make improper performance enhancing substances available to their athletes, or to cheat in the athletic competition.

The pressures are real and, especially in moments of weakness, can seem overpowering, particularly when they are coupled with opportunities and rationalizations.

Opportunities

Businesses concerned with protecting themselves attempt to eliminate the opportunities for unethical behavior by establishing controls. However, those controls are not often foolproof. In one seminar of fraud investigators, the instructor divided the participants in half. The participants in the room, depending on which side of the room they were seated, were required either to create a set of controls to protect some valuable asset of a fictitious company or to perpetrate a fraud associated with that asset that would not be detected by the controls. In every instance, the fraud investigators were successful in devising a scheme that would not be detected by the controls. Ethical persons will devote their attention to eliminating or at least controlling the opportunities for unethical behavior to occur.

Employment in a non-corporate environment likewise presents opportunities to engage in unethical behavior. While controls are often established to measure and monitor performance, there are opportunities to override those controls. The culture of the organization can contribute to a relaxation of official standards of conduct. To cite a personal example, many years ago I served in the military. Tests were administered to measure the readiness of the troops. On one occasion several hundred of us were assembled in a room to sit for an examination. Blank pieces of paper and pencils were distributed to all. We were asked to place our names at the top of the page and then write the numbers 1 through 25 (or so) down the left hand side of the page. Then someone at the front of the room read aloud the multiple choice answers, "number one, C", "number two, D", "number three, B", and so forth, and we were asked to write down the answers on our test sheets. To this day, I do not know what we were being "tested" on and how I performed on the exam.

Rationalizations

Unlimited imagination allows for unlimited rationalizations. But these are some of the common ones:

- Everybody does it.
- They owe it to me.
- When times are better, I will pay it back.
- That's just the way business is done.
- It may be unethical, but it's probably legal.
- I don't expect to get caught.
- I must do it out of a duty of loyalty to ___ (my boss, my friend, my company, my union).
- I can't be held responsible if I'm just doing what my boss tells me to do.
- It's a big company, and the loss won't be felt.
- It's what's best for the company.
- That rule doesn't apply to me in this particular situation.
- I'm not sure that's what the rule means.

- It depends on what your definition of ___ is.
- The good I do certainly outweighs this.
- They told me to do "whatever it takes" to get it done.
- He had to know I was bluffing.
- It's for a good cause.
- I pay my fair share of taxes.

Each of these rationalizations "allows" a person to engage in behavior that demonstrates a lack of integrity. Unfortunately, the pressures are often intense and require immediate attention. The better we are at anticipating the opportunities to rationalize, the more likely it is that we will be prepared to manage them. The person who desires to live a life of integrity should be aware of the rationalizations and be prepared to avoid using them.

Being Aware of Weak Moments

Being aware of and prepared for weak moments can also be key to avoiding improper behavior. Idleness, fatigue, anger, fear, pressure, and passion can contribute to moments of weakness. During these moments of weakness, the rationalizations can seem more logical. Take, for example, "I pay my fair share of taxes." This logic may seem more credible the closer a person gets to the date when the taxes are due. Ability to control thoughts and actions is critical to success in engaging in honorable behavior. Adam Smith wrote,

> " We need to practice focusing our thoughts on the dignity of what we do when we are at our best, and we need to help those who work with us to do the same thing."
>
> — Tom Morris

The man who acts according to the rules of
perfect prudence, of strict justice, and of proper
benevolence, may be said to be perfectly virtuous.
But the most perfect knowledge of those rules
will not alone enable him to act in this manner:
his own passions are very apt to mislead him;
sometimes to drive him and sometimes to seduce
him to violate all the rules which he himself, in all
his sober and cool hours, approves of. The most
perfect knowledge, if it is not supported by the
most perfect self-command, will not always enable
him to do his duty.[5]

Among the most common pressures affected by weak
moments is financial pressure. A careful reexamination of
the list of rationalizations
above reveals that most
of them can easily be
associated with financial
pressures. When financial
issues are not managed
responsibly, many of the

" Creditors are a kind of People, that have the sharpest Eyes and Ears, as well as the best Memories of any in the World." – *Benjamin Franklin*

negative emotions begin to control. The example previously
cited of Betty, the bookkeeper, is a classic example. Living from
paycheck to paycheck when financial demands are excessive
takes away contentment and peace of mind. The first century
B.C. Roman philosopher Horace, son of a former slave, insisted,
"He will always be a slave who does not know how to live upon
a little."[6] Alexander Pope seems to have completed Horace's
thought: "Whatever makes man a slave takes half his worth
away."[7] Living within one's means makes it easier to find the

freedom to follow through with ethical resolutions.

Sometimes financial pressures bear down on business entities and create pressures on employees to act improperly for the sake of the company and its owners and officers. Consider these examples:

- Frank is CEO of a fast growing "dot com" business called TrendUp.com. With its steady growth in earnings, TrendUp.com's stock prices have continued to rise. After fifteen quarters of earnings growth, it appears that the demand for their product is leveling off. Out of fear of a decrease in the value of the company's stock, Frank encourages distributors of their product to take extra product as if actual sales had occurred, but secretly agrees that the distributors do not have to pay for the product until the distributors have sold it. That way, TrendUp.com gets to book their sales early in spite of what generally accepted accounting principles say about this practice. TrendUp.com's stock will continue its rise as long as they can pump up the earnings without getting caught.

- Roberta is the primary shareholder of a financial institution. Certain levels of equity must be maintained in order to comply with government regulations. In order to satisfy the earnings requirements, she and her accountant defer certain expenses on the income statement by capitalizing them on the balance sheet.

Sometimes weak moments affect behaviors even when financial considerations are not a factor. Consider these examples.

- Rick works long hours to support his young family. Sometimes late in the day, he and others get tired and a little "punchy" around the office. Rick likes to have fun, but occasionally the subject matter of his humor gets out of hand. He makes a comment to a female employee in the office that is off color and can potentially be construed as a form of sexual harassment.

- Fred needs an A grade on his research paper. Fred is highly capable, but time pressures do not permit him to spend the requisite time to do the independent research and to write an effective paper. His fraternity maintains a file of excellent research papers that have been submitted in the past. One of them happens to be on target. He submits that instead of creating his own.

- Janet is a young professional with an accounting firm. During the summer months when they are not as busy as at other times, Janet gets involved in playing games and engaging in time-wasting activities that do not contribute to her betterment or that of the firm.

Associating with Good People

"Associate yourself with men of good quality if you esteem your own reputation, for it is better to be alone than in bad company."[8] These words are found in George Washington's "Rules of Civility," which he copied from a translated version of a French book of etiquette dating back to the sixteenth century. Associating with good company is one of the important keys to enabling us to follow through with our ethical resolutions. The reason? As Philip Dormer Stanhope, Earl of Chesterfield, said, "Every man becomes, to a certain degree, what the people he generally converses with are."[9]

Very often those with whom we associate in a work environment do not share our values. Caution is therefore warranted. Deciding the extent of associations with others requires a good deal of discernment that is logically derived through

> **"He that resolves to deal with none but honest men must leave off dealing."**
>
> – *Thomas Fuller*

experience and investigation. Trust in these relationships can only be developed over time. Those relationships that encourage behaviors consistent with personal standards should be preferred.

Persons who choose to engage in business relationships while following ethical principles soon discover that others who do not adhere to those same principles may seek to take advantage of them. The best way to avoid this problem is to associate with those who merit trust. If we learn that others lack appropriate ethical standards, we can plan for the risk by increasing our controls or by eliminating the associations. There are plenty of opportunities to respond in kind and, in so doing, to lower personal standards. For the ethically excellent, that is not the correct solution.

Unique Pitfalls of Employment

Experience dictates that no matter what someone does for a living, there are unique opportunities that can lead to unethical behavior. Here are just a few:

- Professional firms are often in a position to refer outside services to their clients. The provider who gets referred is often in a position to refer business back to them. When that occurs, are the clients' best interests being served?

- Medical doctors refer patients to laboratories and outside therapists. Medical doctors have been known to have financial interests in those outside entities.

- Medical doctors perform services, then bill insurance providers. Misstating the nature and extent of the services provided is a common problem.

- Persons working in construction sometimes accumulate "excess" materials from the job sites. Those materials have been paid for by the owner of the property. Where do the excess materials end up? Sometimes they end up in the personal residences or inventories of the builders.

It is critical that persons wanting to be ethically excellent take the time to examine their own employment and consider the unique ethical pitfalls of their position. Then they should realize that what is considered common practice may not be the best practice.

Whistleblowing

One of the most difficult challenges in the workplace is shedding some of the street logic with which most of us grow up. Consider some of the ideas that may have been acquired from relationships with friends and family. "Blood is thicker than water" is a maxim that suggests it is appropriate to prefer family over others. "It's wrong to tell on others" suggests a need to be loyal to friends. Rules in the workplace differ, largely because street logic can tend to contribute to unfairness. These kinds of situations create some of the most common and most challenging ethical dilemmas in the workplace. Consider a few examples:

- Sam works in an office. He observes some others who do not seem to be carrying their weight. They spend a lot of time talking, playing games on the computer, and communicating with friends in Internet "chat rooms." Sam is not their supervisor. The supervisor either is not paying attention or does not seem to care. Should Sam report his co-workers' wastefulness to a superior?

- Matthew works in sales. He is encouraged to follow practices that seem to be deceptive. He knows the practices are widespread. Should he voice his concerns? And if so, to whom?

- Brad works in engineering. His employer is engaged in providing services under multiple contracts, some of which are with the government. Some of the contracts are based on a fixed fee, and others are on a "cost-plus" basis, according to which his employer gets paid based on the hours worked on the contract times an hourly rate. Brad keeps careful and honest records of his time spent on the various contracts. He has been asked to alter his time records to push time into the cost-plus contracts because the company has "maxed out" on the fixed-fee contract. This way the company can continue to make money all of the time. What should Brad do?

Sam, Matthew, and Brad have some characteristics in common. Assuming each considers himself an ethical person, each has resolved to follow through with his ethical resolutions, and each is now faced with an ethical dilemma. The range of seriousness of the dilemmas, however, appears significant. Brad's dilemma is particularly serious, since the alleged activities are illegal. Sam, Matthew, and Brad must decide whether and how to react. They have at least five choices.[10]

1. They can knowingly participate in the improper behavior. In the case of Sam, he risks the consequences of participating in wasteful practices. That could mean termination. He avoids the

negative repercussions from his fellow workers.
Matthew is employed by a company that seems
to endorse deceptive sales practices; engaging
in improper behavior would appear to carry no
consequences at least from his employer. Brad,
on the other hand, runs the risk of being indicted
along with others in his company on charges
of fraud against the government. Viewed from
an ethical perspective, going along with and
participating in these three forms of unethical
behavior results in all three living contrary to their
ethical principles, and, therefore, losing their sense
of integrity.[11]

2. They can choose not to participate, but do nothing
    to report the improper behavior. This is often the
    least risky response, particularly in situations where
    there is no formal reporting process that allows
    someone to disclose the perceived wrongdoing.
    Nevertheless, wrongdoing observed but not
    reported may result in negative consequences to
    the observer. But, again, viewed from an ethical
    prospective, a selfish concern for the consequences
    may not be the ethically correct motivation.[12]

3. On their own, they can try to stop the improper
    behavior. This approach is appealing because it is
    a consistent expression of the individual's ethical
    convictions, and it is quick. Unfortunately, one
    person's attempt to stop the behavior in this
    fashion may lack the power to cause change.

When a person acts alone in this process, it is easier for an employer to include dismissal of the whistleblower as part of the solution.[13]

4. They can report the offense through the procedures established by the employer. Particularly when the company offers anonymous reporting opportunities, this can be an effective way of solving the problem without unfair consequences to the innocent accuser. Reporting through the established channels is a demonstration of loyalty to the employer. In the cases of Matthew and Brad, however, it is unlikely that the superiors are interested in hearing the complaint. In fact, if they are condoning and engaging in dishonest activities, they will probably be interested in determining the source of the anonymous tip and eliminating that person. Clearly, Matthew and Brad should be carefully considering whether it is appropriate for them to continue their employment regardless of the outcome. Preparing to follow through with their ethical resolutions in this case may require them to quit and seek employment elsewhere.[14]

5. They can disclose the wrongdoing outside normal reporting processes. This might involve reporting directly to top management, the board of directors, union leadership, law enforcement, or the press.[15] Studies suggest that in many instances whistleblowing of this sort will probably result in termination or demotion.[16]

The choices these three persons make will be influenced by several factors: their personal values regarding what constitutes right and wrong behavior, their interpretation of the facts surrounding the ethical dilemmas, their understanding of the seriousness of these apparent dilemmas, their assessment of the likely consequences of their decisions, their perceived ability to deal with the consequences, and their level of courage and commitment to follow through with their ethical resolutions.[17]

Richard T. DeGeorge has offered certain criteria regarding when it is morally permissible to blow the whistle on an employer.

1. When the firm, through its product or policy, will do serious and considerable harm to the public, whether in the person of the user of its product, an innocent bystander, or the general public, whistleblowing is appropriate.

2. Once employees identify a serious threat to the user of a product or to the general public, they should report it to their immediate superior and make their moral concern known. Unless they do so, the act of whistleblowing is not clearly justifiable.

3. If an employee's immediate superior does nothing effective about the concern or complaint, the employee should exhaust the internal procedures and possibilities within the firm. This usually will involve taking the matter up the managerial ladder and, if necessary-and possible-to the board of directors.

4. The whistleblower must have, or have accessible, documented evidence that would convince a reasonable, impartial observer that the employee's view of the situation is correct, and that the company's product or practice poses a serious and likely danger to the public or to the user of the product.

5. The employee must have good reasons to believe that by going public the necessary changes will be brought about. The chance of being successful must be worth the risk one takes and the danger to which one is exposed.[18]

The above steps present significant challenges. Among these are the determination of whether the evidence of wrongdoing is credible, whether the alleged offense is significant, and whether by going public some "good" will be achieved. These steps are an important part of the process.[19]

I discussed earlier Lawrence Kohlberg's Levels of Moral Development. The level of a person's moral development - pre-conventional, conventional, or post-conventional - will affect his determination as to what constitutes ethical behavior and how to undertake a course of action in dealing with ethical dilemmas. The higher the level of moral development, the more likely a person will recognize behavior that has ethical consequences, particularly behavior that has negative consequences to others.

A word of caution is necessary. When taken to its extreme, a culture that places high priority on identifying evidences of improper behavior runs the risk of creating a culture where there is a lack of trust. An organization in which there is a major emphasis on looking for evidences of misconduct and engaging in investigations of fellow employees becomes an unpleasant place to work. Such an environment developed when Nero ruled Rome or Stalin ruled the Soviet Union.[20] Peter Drucker warned, "Under whistleblowing, under the regime of the informer, no mutual trust, no interdependencies, and no ethics are possible."[21] The primary focus of any organization should be the accomplishment of its objectives - profits, service, development, and care. While all should keep their eyes wide open, care must be taken to keep their eyes on the worthy objectives of the organization. Those committed to honorable behavior must remember that they must be committed to competence and diligence, as outlined in Choice 1.

Commitment

Preparing to follow through with ethical resolutions requires making a personal commitment to the principles and causes that are important. The historian Josephus described an interesting example of commitment to principles. Stephen L. Carter relates it in his book *Integrity*.

> **" He does not believe that does not live according to his belief."** – *Thomas Fuller*

> When the Roman general Petronius was ordered during the first century to erect a statue of the Emperor Caligula in the Temple in Jerusalem, tens of thousands of unarmed Jews protested, baring their throats and insisting that they would rather die than become idolators. After extended negotiations, Petronius pronounced himself

sufficiently moved by their courage that he could
not carry out his orders. He wrote to the Emperor
saying that honor would not allow him to place the
statue in the Temple.[22]

While "baring our throats" is rarely the requirement in standing
up for what is perceived to be right, the personal sacrifices at
the moments of confrontation can be significant. These are the
moments when we are hoping that our understanding of the
facts is based on a thorough and critical analysis. These are the
moments when we wish we were not living from paycheck to
paycheck.

We equip ourselves to demonstrate commitment to
ethical excellence in the difficult moments by meeting the
ethical requirements of the lesser challenging moments. As
Baldwin Brown wrote,
"Temperament we are born
with, character we have
to make; and that not in
the grand moments . . .
but in the daily, quiet paths

**" A talent if formed in stillness,
a character in the world's
torrent."**

– Johann Wolfgang von Goethe

of pilgrimage."[23] Meeting the requirements during the lesser
moments builds confidence in an ability to handle the challenges
of the greater ones.

We equip ourselves to demonstrate commitment to ethical
excellence by developing a reputation for ethical excellence
among those with whom we associate. When others expect
a high standard of excellence, it is easier to continue to
demonstrate it. Further, we should be willing to discuss our
standards of ethical excellence with others and involve them in
the deliberative processes. And finally, we should be willing to

take time to remind ourselves of what we believe and how we are committed to act.

Code of Ethics Guidance Regarding Following Through With Ethical Resolutions

From the professions:

Accounting: Preamble: "The Principles call for an unswerving commitment to honorable behavior, even at the sacrifice of personal advantage."

From the corporate world:

ExxonMobil Corporation: "Regardless of how much difficulty we encounter or pressure we face in performing our jobs, no situation can justify the willful violation of these policies."

Wal-Mart: "As Wal-Mart Associates and Directors we must: . . . Never act unethically – even if someone else instructs you to do so."

Microsoft: "Delivering on our mission requires great people who are bright, creative, and energetic, and who share the following values: . . . Accountable for commitments, results, and quality to customers, shareholders, partners, and employees."

Code of Ethics Guidance
Regarding Whistleblowing

From the corporate world:

ExxonMobil Corporation: "No action may be taken or threatened against any employee for asking questions, voicing concerns, or making complaints or suggestions in conformity with the procedures described above, unless the employee acts with willful disregard of the truth."

Wal-Mart: "Immediately raise any concern that you or others may have about possible violations of this Statement of Ethics or any Wal-Mart policy."

Home Depot: "The Open Door Policy is intended to create an atmosphere that encourages Associates to voice concerns, express doubts, discuss problems, ask questions, make observations and offer suggestions about workplace issues." "Associates have a duty to report suspected wrongdoing and should do so without fear of retaliation. The Company will not tolerate any retaliation or threats of retaliation against anyone that reports in good faith a violation or suspected violation of the law, any Company Policy or the Business Code of Conduct and Ethics."

Citigroup Inc.: "Employees and other Citigroup representatives who suspect or become aware of violations of law, regulation or Citigroup policy should communicate their suspicions to the appropriate internal representatives. A telephone hotline number has been established for this purpose."

Boeing: "They will promptly report any illegal or unethical conduct to management or other appropriate authorities."

The Kroger Co.: "All associates are obligated to report to the company any inappropriate use of company assets, violations of law or this policy, or other similar improprieties, and are encouraged to report any concerns they have regarding any possible improper conduct."

Berkshire Hathaway Inc.: [Steps in dealing with suspected Code of Business Conduct and Ethics violations] 1. "Make sure you have all the facts." 2. "Ask yourself: What specifically am I being asked to do? Does it seem unethical or improper? Use your judgment and common sense. If something seems unethical or improper, it probably is." 3. "Clarify your responsibility and role . . . It may help to get others involved and discuss the problem." 4. "Discuss the problem with your supervisor." 5. "Seek help from Company resources. . . . discuss it locally with your office manager or your human resources manager." 6. "You may report ethical violations in confidence without fear of retaliation." 7. "Ask first, act later."

Notes

1   Thomas Paine, "The American Crisis" as quoted in William J. Bennett, *Our Sacred Honor* (Nashville, Tennessee: Broadman & Holman Publishers, 1997), 37-38.

2   Autobiography, *The Works of Benjamin Franklin* (New York: G.P. Putman's Sons, 1904), Vol 1:197.

3   William H. Shaw and Vincent Barry, *Moral Issues in Business* (Belmont, California: Wadsworth, 1999), 5-6.

4   Douglas Chismar, "Vice and Virtue in Everyday (Business) Life," *Journal of Business Ethics* 29 (2001): 170.

5   Adam Smith, *The Theory of Moral Sentiments* (Indianapolis: Liberty Fund, 1984), 237.

6   As quoted in Ted Goodman, ed., *The Forbes Book of Business Quotations* (New York: Black Dog & Leventhal Publishers, Inc., 1997), 774.

7   As quoted in Goodman, ed. *The Forbes Book of Business Quotations*, 775.

8   From George Washington's "Rules of Civility" which he copied from a translated version of a French book of etiquette, dating back to the sixteenth century. As quoted in Bennett, *Our Sacred Honor*, 154.

9   As quoted in Tom Morris, *If Aristotle Ran General Motors* (New York: Henry Holt and Company, 1997), 162.

10   David L. McLain and John P. Keenan, "Risk, Information, and the Decision about Response to Wrongdoing in an Organization," *Journal of Business Ethics* 19 (1999): 257-258.

11   McLain and Keenan, "Risk, Information, and the Decision," 257.

12   McLain and Keenan, "Risk, Information, and the Decision," 257.

13   McLain and Keenan, "Risk, Information, and the Decision," 257.

14   McLain and Keenan, "Risk, Information, and the Decision," 257.

15   McLain and Keenan, "Risk, Information, and the Decision," 257.

16   One such study in the U.S. "found that 90 percent of people who had gone public with their concerns had been fired or demoted or had quit." From David Olive, *Just Rewards: The Case for Ethical Reform in Business* (Toronto: Key Porter Books, 1987), 132.

17   McLain and Keenan, "Risk, Information, and the Decision," 257.

18   Richard T. DeGeorge, *Business Ethics, Fourth Edition* (Englewood Cliffs, New Jersey: Prentice Hall, 1995), 231-236.

19   DeGeorge, *Business Ethics,* 231-236.

20   Olive, *Just Rewards,* 131.

21   Olive, *Just Rewards*, 131.

22   Stephen L. Carter, *Integrity* (New York: BasicBooks, 1996), 15.

23   As quoted in Ted Goodman, ed., *The Forbes Book of Business Quotations*, 131.

Text Box Footnotes

Pliny, "Let honor be to us..." Ted Goodman, ed., *The Forbes Book of Business Quotations* (New York: Black Dog & Leventhal Publishers, Inc., 1997), 412.

Max DePree, "Being faithful to a set..." *Atlanta Journal Constitution,* December 11, 1989, sec. B, 6.

Williams & Houch, "The choice is ours to make..." Oliver F. Williams & John W. Houck, eds. *A Virtuous Life in Business* (Lanham, Maryland, Rowman & Littlefield Publishers, Inc., 1992), 86.

Tom Morris, "We need to practice…" Tom Morris, *If Aristotle Ran General Motors* (New York: Henry Holt and Company, 1997), 168.

Benjamin Franklin, "Creditors are the kind…" Benjamin Franklin giving advice to a young tradesman in a letter to "A.B." as quoted in William J. Bennett, *Our Sacred Honor* (Nashville: Broadman & Holman Publishers, 1997), 284.

Thomas Fuller, "He that resolves…" Ted Goodman, ed., *The Forbes Book of Business Quotations* (New York: Black Dog & Leventhal Publishers, Inc., 1997), 408.

Thomas Fuller, "He does not believe…" World of Quotes.com, http:// www.world of quotes.com/author/Thomas-Fuller/1/.

von Goethe, "A talent is formed…" Inspirational-Quotes.org, http://wwwInspirational-quotes.org.

Choose to Be an Impartial Spectator of Personal Character and Conduct

" There is no greater delight than to be conscious of sincerity on self-examination."[1] - *Confucius*

To illustrate the final choice, I once again return to Victor Hugo's *Les Miserables*. Following his release from prison, Jean Valjean is falsely accused of stealing a coin from a young boy and is pursued for that crime and for the crime of violating his parole. Valjean has successfully avoided detection from the persistent police inspector, Javert. Another character, Champmathieu, has been caught in a petty violation of the law, and is falsely identified as the fugitive, Jean Valjean. Valjean is informed of the impending prosecution of Champmathieu for Valjean's alleged crimes of the distant past. Valjean faces a dilemma. Should he admit to being the real Valjean and face a return to prison in order to spare the "luckless" Champmathieu an undeserved fate? Jean Valjean anguishes over his decision. Hugo describes his reflections in these words:

> Monsieur Madeleine [Jean Valjean] did not hesitate
> to sacrifice the first consideration to the second -
> his personal security to his moral principles.
> He had, it seems, concluded, after the manner
> of saints and sages, that his first duty was not
> to himself. But no situation like the present had
> ever before arisen. Never had the two principles
> governing the life of this unfortunate man ["to
> conceal his true identity and sanctify his life, and to
> escape from men and find his way back to God"]
> been brought so sharply into conflict.[2]

> After a little while, despite himself, he resumed that
> sombre dialogue in which he was both speaker
> and audience, saying things he did not wish to say,
> hearing things he did not wish to hear, yielding to
> that mysterious power which said to him, "Reflect,"
> as two thousand years before it had said to another
> condemned man, "Take up thy Cross!" At that point,
> and in order that we may be fully understood, we
> must interpolate an observation. It is certain that
> we talk to ourselves; there is no thinking person
> who has not done so. It may indeed be said that
> the word is never a more splendid mystery than
> when it travels in a man's mind from thought to
> conscience and back again to thought.[3]

> It was his most melancholy destiny that he
> could achieve sanctity in the eyes of God only by
> returning to degradation in the eyes of men.[4]

> Whether he turned right or left the end was a
> sepulchre, the death of one thing or the other,
> happiness or virtue.[5]

The reflections Hugo attributes to Jean Valjean over his dilemma are illustrative of the careful and principled decision-making that is required of the person who desires to be ethically excellent. Valjean deliberated over the priority of moral principle versus personal security, his duty to others, the uniqueness of his situation, the examples of others who were ethically excellent, and the need to consult and rely on his conscience. Despite the serious consequences of his decision, Valjean, in all these considerations, demonstrates a certain impartiality in his decision-making, Valjean could have reasoned that Champmathieu's life was of little consequence, since he was a former prisoner who contributed little good to society. Instead, Valjean appeared at Champmathieu's trial and announced his identity as the real Jean Valjean.

The Whole Man versus the Self-interested Economic Man

Adam Smith is best known as the founder of modern economics, but he was also a great moralist. In 1759, he published a work entitled *The Theory of Moral Sentiments*. Smith's more famous work is a treatise on economics, entitled *The Wealth of Nations.*[6] It was published in 1776. In these two great works, Smith describes man from two perspectives.

In *The Theory of Moral Sentiments,* Smith describes the "whole man" as a man with a social conscience, a man whose being is self-controlled or limited by sympathy, and a man with the ability to be an "impartial spectator" of his character and conduct. In this work, the themes of hard work and success to benefit others are emphasized, but these are tempered by other character traits.

- "In the race for wealth, and honours, and preferments, he may run as hard as he can and strain every nerve and every muscle, in order to outstrip all his competitors. But if he should jostle, or throw down any of them, the indulgence of the spectators is entirely at an end. It is a violation of fair play, which they cannot admit of."[7]

- "Man was made for action, and to promote by the exertion of his faculties such changes in the external circumstances both of himself and others, as may seem most favourable to the happiness of all."[8]

- "What is the reward most proper for encouraging industry, prudence, and circumspection? Success in every sort of business."[9]

Smith's *The Wealth of Nations* was written at a time when the Industrial Revolution was in its infancy and there were many abuses associated with the British system of mercantilism by its merchant princes. In this work his "economic man" is one who is driven by self-interest. Smith argues that by an "invisible hand" buyers and sellers are motivated to produce and buy goods in a marketplace, and that this process will occur without government interference. As profits are generated, business expands, creating more jobs and increasing the wealth of a nation. The "self-interest" that Smith refers to is a positive feature, one that drives a person to work hard, to produce marketable goods, and, consequently, to improve the quality of his life.

Perhaps it is no surprise that of these two works *The Wealth of Nations* is the one most widely known because of its great impact on economic thought. It is an attack on the free trade restrictions of the British mercantile system. It is an analysis of economic processes, and it considers the relationship between order and freedom.[10] Ethicists, however, have argued, largely without much audience, that Smith intended that the economic man, driven by self-interest, should also be driven to exercise prudence and benevolence, therefore bettering himself in order to improve society.[11] A careful reading of the many characteristics of the whole man in *The Theory of Moral Sentiments* suggests that Smith recognized that the whole man could be properly involved in the activities of the economic man. Without any evidence that Smith ever intended to withdraw his opinions of the earlier work, it seems logical that his descriptions of the economic man in his later work should not be taken out of the whole man context. Any inference that Smith intended that the economic man be a self-serving or selfish man, rather than a man whose self-interests contribute to the well-being of the community, would be false.[12]

Impartial Spectators

One of the most difficult challenges we all face is to see ourselves as we really are - to be able to "step out of our own skin" and determine whether we, as individual human beings, are acting consistently with what we perceive are moral principles. When we fail to be impartial spectators of our own character and conduct, we often deceive ourselves into believing that our actions are right, when, in fact, they may not be.

Being impartial spectators of character and conduct involves a careful evaluation of how we will react to alternative choices. A careful process of choosing considers which of the alternatives is most consistent with a sense of right. It involves sorting out evidences of compartmentalization within our lives. It is easy to rationalize away the applicability of principled behavior in different circumstances. Differences in the "private self" and the "public self" may be less than we suspect they should be.[13]

To become impartial spectators, we must remove ourselves from our "own natural station," and view situations from a distance.[14] Preferences, loyalties, values, fears, and angers can act to influence what is perceived to be right. While some of these can be good influences, they sometimes cloud perceptions, and even "excuse" us from feeling any need to assess the rightness of situations. People are generally not at their best when negative emotions are impacting their state of mind and their ability to make correct decisions. Being impartial implies being able to make decisions that are substantially free from the personal emotions that affect decisions. When we are not free of these emotions, later on, when the passions that affected those decisions have subsided, the reasons for making the choices do not seem as credible as they once did.[15]

That is not to say, however, that the absence of emotions is a good character trait. Those who lack emotions tend to be less sensitive to the needs and desires of others. Some decisions are best made with a clearer understanding of what it must feel like to be affected by a decision. Having the ability to feel emotions logically contributes to a more humane treatment of others and to a more complete understanding of the circumstances affecting a proper judgment.

Deciding *when* to be impartial spectators of character and conduct can affect individual ability to succeed in this characteristic. Consider an actual example of a discussion involving ten senior vice-presidents of a large U.S. corporation meeting to discuss their code of ethics and specifically how they can make it more effective. One participant comments, "The real problem, as I see it, is whether we do the right thing when issues arise or do what will mean more profit. It's okay to have a code of ethics, but we are first of all in business to make money. If the profit is rolling in, we can afford to put our values into operation."[16]

Analysis of Personal Conduct

Being an impartial spectator of character and conduct involves looking at personal conduct, not compared with a neighbor or friend, but rather compared with what is right and best. Socrates warned that the unexamined life was not worth living.[17] Seeing ourselves as we really are often requires a more deliberative process than the instantaneous judgments we typically make. James Cash Penney began his highly successful store by adopting a philosophy known as "The Penney Idea." It consists of seven objectives, the seventh of which is "to test our every policy, method, and act in this wise: 'Does it square with what is right and just?'"[18] Frequently asking ourselves whether our thoughts, words, and actions are right and just is precisely what is required in this deliberative process.

Careful examination of conduct is required at all stages of activities. Socrates said, "It is desirable that thought should rule before an act, during the act, and after the act: before the act, so that it will not be mean and hurtful; during the act, so that it does not cause a nuisance; and after the act, so that it may be followed up and it may be known what it has led to, and its beginning may be assessed by its end."[19]

> " I do not try to dance better than anyone else. I only try to dance better than myself."
>
> – Mikhail Baryshnikov

The analysis of personal conduct should include asking questions such as:

- "In doing this, am I becoming the kind of person I want to be?"[20]
- When the light of day shines on this, will it appear to be the appropriate decision?
- Is this my best effort?
- How might my personal preferences and emotions be influencing my decision?

Deciding on the appropriateness of conduct should involve an evaluation of the consequences of that conduct. A proper and thorough evaluation of conduct will consider the likely effects of our acts on ability to reason, to appreciate that which is good, and to abhor that which is bad. The perceived problem is that it takes time to evaluate, and time is a precious commodity. Think about the time saved in not having to take corrective action on the mistakes of the past!

Conflicts of Interest

In a business setting, conflicts of interest frequently make it difficult to exercise impartial behavior. A conflict of interest is a situation where the interests (i.e. desires or loyalties) of a *person* (or his or her family or friends or enemies) and the interests of the *position* or *office* the person holds are different, making it difficult for the person to discharge his duties as he should.[21] The following examples should be helpful to illustrate this simple definition:

- Jan is the City Manager for Maple City. She determines which insurance company writes the policies for health insurance for the city employees. Her brother-in-law owns an insurance agency that handles health insurance. Placing the insurance with her brother-in-law's agency would represent a conflict of interest.

Jan's example emphasizes that certain relationships tend to hinder or make difficult a person's ability to perform the duties of her office. In the case of Jan's placement of the health insurance, her brother-in-law's insurance agency may be the best choice for the city. Her best professional judgment may lead her to that decision. Nevertheless, the conflict exists. The fact that Jan is employed in a governmental position further complicates her choice, since some positions require an especially high standard of independent action. Jan's actions must not violate the special trust that the public expects of persons who are elected and of persons who serve under the direction of elected officials.

- Jack is a store manager for Friendly Grocers. He is charged with the responsibility of hiring an assistant manager for his store. Out of a concern for his own position, Jack may be inclined to hire someone slightly less qualified than he is.

Dealing with business conflicts of interest that pose a threat to one's job, title, or compensation represents particular challenges. In Jack's case, for the sake of preserving his own position, might he not be inclined to hire someone that is slightly less qualified for fear of having a highly qualified person take over his position? Jack's best interests and those of his employer might be different. This conflict might best be resolved by turning the hiring decision over to another.

- Bill is Director of Corporate Security at Giant Steel. He determines which security guard service is hired. ABC Guard Service is willing to pay Bill personally (i.e. under the table) $10,000 per year if Bill hires ABC each year and does not require a bidding process. To the extent that Bill has an interest in receiving the under-the-table payment, he has created a conflict of interest.

Unlike the previous examples of conflicts of interest, the example of a simple bribe illustrates how conflicts can be created from less than noble motivations. Pure greed, coupled with an opportunity, although unsolicited, may result in a serious violation of the law. Bribery has become a standard practice in many parts of the world, and can constitute a significant cost of doing business. In China, for example, it is estimated that three percent to five percent of the operating costs of doing business go to bribes or gifts to the government.[22]

- Bart is a senior official in a government bureaucracy. The size of his organization affects his title, his compensation, and even his ability to keep his job. The interests of those whom the bureaucracy serves are efficient operations at a minimum cost. Cutting back on the size of the organization represents a conflict for Bart.

These types of conflicts are particularly difficult to deal with, in part because traditional practices are widely accepted and the number of people involved in the decision-making process is significant. When a person's job is at stake, the temptation is particularly great.

- Mary is a medical doctor. As part of her professional responsibilities, she serves on a panel that evaluates the behavior of other physicians in cases where a lawsuit has been brought against a doctor or hospital. The recommendations of her panel are used by courts in evaluating the credibility of the claims brought by lawyers in attempting to reach a settlement. If her panel continually recognizes fault with the doctors, how will the members of her panel be viewed by others in her profession? How will large damage awards against doctors affect her professional liability insurance premiums? The selfish motivation is to protect her profession.

Mary and the members of her medical panel are faced with a significant ethical challenge. It is easy to rationalize actions that require a level of professional judgment, believing that alternative choices can be deemed acceptable. The members of this panel, no doubt, are aware of the crisis that the medical profession is facing in the cost of insurance premiums. These panel members may be motivated to do their part in curbing those costs. They are in a position to make a difference, at least in their own community.

- The law firm of Williams & Hanna is employed by a client to defend a large lawsuit. They normally charge professional fees that generate an average rate per hour of $265. They consider themselves qualified to do the work and have the personnel necessary to staff the job, but the client is not willing to pay the standard hourly rates of the firm. The client wants a ten percent discount off standard hourly rates. The partner in charge of the potential client wants the work. She is tempted to pad the bill with excess hours to make up for the potential deficiency in what the firm believes are reasonably priced services.

Pressures within professional firms to maintain hourly rates and achieve profit goals can result in unethical activities. The bill padding described in this example is almost impossible to detect. Promoting personal interests typically is the motive behind this activity. Those who are asked to cooperate may act out of self-preservation.

- Greg has worked as a production manager at a mining company for twenty-eight years. Greg has purchased shares of the company's stock that are traded on the open market, and has done quite well with his investment. He expects to retire in three years and will be dependent on his investment in the company stock. He discovers that new estimates of the available mineral deposits that the company mines appear to have decreased unexpectedly. It is anticipated that when the public learns of the revised mineral deposit assessments the trading price of the company stock will drop significantly. He is tempted to unload a significant number of his shares before the market learns of the problem.

Having inside information that will affect the value of a stock investment creates a significant temptation to buy or sell. As insiders buy or sell their stock, the persons on the other side of the transaction will be detrimentally affected by stock values that are about to change.

Praise Versus Praiseworthy Behavior

Identifying success is often a difficult task. Honors are awarded based on perceived achievements in academic excellence, profitability in business, accumulation of wealth, and winning in games. Yet, many achievements can be merely "resemblances to merit"[23] when less than best effort, cheating, and improper influence contribute to the results. Benjamin Franklin instructed, "What you seem to be, be really."[24] Unfortunately, too often the perceived success and resulting honor are unearned. Consider these examples:

" **The shortest and surest way to live with honor in the world is to be in reality what we would appear to be; all human virtues increase and strengthen themselves by the practice and experience of them.**" *– Socrates*

- Mike's friends in their chemistry class have discovered that their professor tests the class using a book that is available on the Internet. A copy of the book is now circulating among students in the class and has proven to be a reliable source for identifying material on the exam. The chemistry teacher grades on the curve. Mike reasons that since most others in the class are taking advantage of the secret testing materials, he places himself at a competitive disadvantage by not using the book. He looks at the book and receives an A in the class.

- Diane is applying for a job as a sales representative that requires five years of prior experience in sales. While she does not have a lot of sales experience, she has confidence that she has the requisite skills to do the job. She decides to pad her resume by

falsely representing her employment experience
to increase her chances of landing the job. Diane
receives an opportunity that she has not earned.

- Barbara is proud of her son and wants him to
  have many opportunities to succeed. Barbara is
  the PTA President at the local high school. Barbara
  occasionally applies pressure on the faculty to
  give her son opportunities, such as leadership
  appointments, and to relax rules on testing to yield
  grades that he would not have otherwise earned.
  Other students lose out on opportunities they have
  earned.

- The compensation structure at Tom's workplace
  provides for year-end bonus payments based on
  the sales levels achieved. Although others in the
  company contribute to Tom's success, he declines
  to share the credit. Tom receives a bonus he does
  not deserve.

Human beings attach great importance to receiving the praise
of others. The above are all examples of efforts to receive praise
that is unearned. While the world may award honors to such
people, they are not living honorably. When praise is undeserved,
it should be rejected. Ethically excellent persons are those who
focus on being praiseworthy. Adam Smith wisely commented,
"It is only the weakest and most superficial of mankind who
can be much delighted with that praise which they themselves
know to be altogether unmerited. A weak man may sometimes

be pleased with it, but a wise man rejects it upon all occasions."[25] The wise man's preference is to *be* good rather than to just *seem* good.[26]

When we receive honors that we deserve, we can live with dignity and confidence. It allows us to feel a sense of peace - even strength - among all our associates. Deserving honors ought to imply not that we are just doing better than others, but that we are doing our best. An ancient Hindu proverb says, "There is nothing noble in being superior to some other man. The true nobility is in being superior to your previous self."[27] Being less than his best suggests that a person is holding something back in his performance. When he does, he fails to realize the personal development that could have been his. Others affected by his performance receive less than they could have as well.

" Dignity consists not of possessing honors, but in the consciousness that we deserve them." – Aristotle

A Clear and Disciplined Conscience

A clear and disciplined conscience is among the most important of possessions, in part because it contributes to the ability to understand the rightness of feelings and decisions. It prompts us to understand and to be willing to embrace each of the *Ethical Choices*. Conscience has been variously referred to as "a continual feast" (Robert Burton),[28] "the still voice within" (Mahatma Gandhi),[29]

" The heart has arguments with which the logic of the mind is not acquainted." – Blaise Pascal

"man's best friend" (Austin Philps),[30] "a stronger power [and] a more forcible motive" (Adam Smith),[31] "the great judge and arbiter of our conduct" (Adam Smith),[32] and "that little spark of celestial fire" (George Washington's "Rules of Civility").[33] Each of these descriptions contributes to an understanding of conscience. The fact that it is a still voice and a little spark suggests that it is a delicate thing, easily interfered with, and capable of being destroyed. Yet, its description as a feast, a stronger power, a forcible motive, and a great judge and arbiter suggests that conscience is also a great and powerful force.

A clear and disciplined conscience can be nurtured; it can also be diminished. The direction of its development is determined by goodness and obedience to virtues, or a lack thereof. As James Q. Wilson wrote, conscience is nurtured as we take time to think about "what it means to be human and on what terms we can live with ourselves."[34]

Goodness

Finally, it is unlikely that any of us will achieve much success in our efforts to be impartial spectators of our character and conduct - even if we know all the rules - if there is not an abundance of the virtue of goodness in our being. Tom Morris refers to goodness as "a fundamental foundation for human excellence,"[35] and "the soil within which the soul can grow and flourish."[36] Iphicrates characterizes goodness as "true nobility."[37] Goodness is manifest in the simple things that people do - waiting their turn, not driving in the HOV lane if they are alone,

> **" Goodness is the only investment that never fails"**
> — *Henry David Thoreau*

keeping their promises, not cheating on their taxes, picking up a piece of litter, expressing gratitude, and volunteering for a charitable cause. Goodness is also manifested in the big things people do - maintaining integrity and striving for excellence in all aspects of their lives, even the optional ones.

Goodness does not become a part of a person's being unless it becomes part of his nature and disposition. Tom Morris' analogy of goodness being "the soil within which the soul can grow and flourish" suggests that the seeds of virtue, including competence, diligence, confidence, truth, selflessness, and justice, must be planted and nourished in the soil of goodness in order for them to take root and become part of a person's nature. People nourish the seeds of virtue by giving constant attention to their developmental needs and guarding against anything that would impair their growth.

Additional Guidance Regarding Determining Good Character

From the professions:

Education: Preamble: "The educator recognizes the magnitude of the responsibility inherent in the teaching process. The desire for the respect and confidence of one's colleagues, of students, of parents, and of the members of the community provides the incentive to attain and maintain the highest possible degree of ethical conduct."

Engineering: "Engineers . . . conduct themselves honorably, responsibly, ethically, and lawfully so as to enhance the honor, reputation, and usefulness of the profession."

From the corporate world:

Microsoft: "Delivering on our mission requires great people who are bright, creative, and energetic, and who share the following values: . . .Self-critical, questioning, and committed to personal excellence and self-improvement."

Code of Ethics Guidance Regarding Conflicts of Interest

From the professions:

Accounting: Article IV: "Maintain objectivity and be free of conflicts of interest." "The principle of objectivity imposes the obligation to be impartial, intellectually honest, and free of conflicts of interest."

Education: Principle II (Commitment to the Profession): Educators "shall not accept any gratuity, gift, or favor that might impair or appear to influence professional decisions or action."

Engineering: "Engineers shall disclose all known or potential conflicts of interest that could influence or appear to influence their judgment or the quality of their services."

Law: Cannon 9: "A lawyer should avoid even the appearance of professional impropriety."

From the corporate world:

ExxonMobil Corporation: ExxonMobil "employees are expected to avoid any actual or apparent conflict between their own personal interests and the interests of the Corporation."

ExxonMobil Corporation: "It is the policy of ExxonMobile Corporation to base commercial decisions on commercial criteria."

Ford Motor Company: "We expect you to scrupulously avoid even the appearance of a conflict of interest. A simple test: Could your conduct withstand public scrutiny? If your conduct was disclosed to management and reported to the media, would you be able to justify it as lawful and above reproach for a Ford employee? If not, don't do it."

Chevron Texaco: "You have a primary business responsibility to Chevron Texaco and are expected to avoid any activity that may interfere, or have the appearance of interfering, with the performance of this responsibility."

Wal-Mart: "As Wal-Mart Associates and Directors we must: Avoid conflicts of interest between work and personal affairs."

Wal-Mart: "Situations or transactions that create the appearance or perception that you cannot carry out your duties and responsibilities with integrity and impartiality should be avoided."

Wal-Mart: "You should not offer anything of value, directly or through third persons, to anyone (including governmental authorities) to obtain an improper advantage in selling goods and services, conducting financial transactions, or presenting the Company's interests."

Home Depot: "A conflict of interest occurs when an individual's private interest interferes in any way – or even appears to interfere – with the interests of The Home Depot."

Citigroup Inc.: "We establish information barriers, when appropriate, to separate employees engaged in lending, investment banking or merchant banking activities – and who have access to confidential customer information – from employees who trade in securities or engage in investment management."

Citigroup Inc.: "In general, you may not accept gifts or the conveyance of anything of value (including entertainment) from current or prospective Citigroup customers or suppliers."

Citigroup Inc.: "You must be sensitive to any activities, interests or relationships that might interfere with, or even appear to interfere with, your ability to act in the best interests of Citigroup and its customers."

The Kroger Co.: "Bribery in any form is forbidden in the conduct of the business of the company. No company funds are to be used, directly or indirectly, for any bribe, kickback or other unlawful payment."

American International Group, Inc.: "AIG employees must not permit any business decision, such as a decision as to whether AIG will do business with an insured, producer, intermediary, reinsurer, prospect, counterparty or supplier to be influenced, or appear to be influenced, by interests unrelated to AIG. A decision to place AIG business with such entities and the volume of such business must be based solely upon business considerations."

Notes

1   As quoted in http://www.creative quotations.com/one/524a.htm.

2   Victor Hugo (Norman Denny, trans.), *Les Miserables* (New York: Penguin Books, 1976), 209.

3   Hugo, *Les Miserables,* 213.

4   Hugo, *Les Miserables,* 214.

5   Hugo, *Les Miserables,* 221.

6   Its full title is *An Inquiry into the Nature and Cause of the Wealth of Nations.*

7   Adam Smith, *The Theory of Moral Sentiments* (Indianapolis: Liberty Fund, 1984), 83.

8   Smith, *The Theory of Moral Sentiments,* 106.

9   Smith, *The Theory of Moral Sentiments,* 166.

10 "Adam Smith," *The World Book Encyclopedia* (Chicago: World Book-Childcraft International, Inc., 1981) 17: 425.

11 Edward W. Coker, "Adam Smith's Concept of the Social System," *Journal of Business Ethics* 9 (1990):139-142.

12 Coker, "Adam Smith's Concept," 139-142.

13 Rex E. Lee, "Honesty and Integrity," *Brigham Young University Speeches,* September 5, 1995: 17.

14 Smith, *The Theory of Moral Sentiments,* 110.

15 Smith, *The Theory of Moral Sentiments,* 157-158.

16 Oliver F. Williams & John W. Houck (ed.), *A Virtuous Life in Business* (Lanham, Maryland: Rowman & Littlefield Publishers, Inc., 1992), 5-6.

17 As quoted in Stephen L. Carter, *Integrity* (New York: BasicBooks, 1996), 22.

18 David Olive, *Just Rewards: The Case for Ethical Reform in Business* (Toronto: Key Porter Books, 1987), 126.

19 Thomas Cleary (trans.), *Living a Good Life* (Boston: Shambhala, 1997), 40.

20 Tom Morris, *If Aristotle Ran General Motors* (New York: Henry Holt and Company, 1997), 165.

21 Thomas L. Carson, "Conflicts of Interest," *Journal of Business Ethics* 13 (1994): 388.

22 K. Pennar, P. Galuska, D. Lindoff and R. Jesurum, "The Destructive Costs of Greasing Palms," *Business Week*, Dec. 6, 1993: 133-138.

23 Hugo, *Les Miserables*, 64.

24 Benjamin Franklin, as quoted in William J. Bennett, *Our Sacred Honor,* (Nashville, Tennessee: Broadman & Holman, 1997), 146.

25 Smith, *The Theory of Moral Sentiments*, 117.

26 Sallust, referring to Cato: "He preferred to be, rather than to seem, good" as quoted in Tom Morris, *If Aristotle Ran General Motors*, 209.

27 As quoted in Tom Morris, *If Aristotle Ran General Motors*, 55.

28 As quoted in http://www.quoteworld.org/author.php.

29 As quoted in http://www.worldofquotes.com/topic/Conscience.

30 As quoted in http://www.quotelady.com/subjects/conscience.html.

31 Smith, *The Theory of Moral Sentiments*, 137.

32 Smith, *The Theory of Moral Sentiments*, 137.

33 From George Washington's "Rules of Civility" which he copied from a translated version of a French book of etiquette, dating back to the sixteenth century, as quoted in William J. Bennett, *Our Sacred Honor*, 155.

34 James Q. Wilson, *The Moral Sense* (New York: The Free Press, 1993), 33.

35 Morris, *If Aristotle Ran General Motors*, 123.

36 Morris, *If Aristotle Ran General Motors,* 117.

37 Morris, *If Aristotle Ran General Motors,* 123.

Text Box Footnotes

Baryshnikov, "I do not try to..." As quoted in Tom Morris, *If Aristotle Ran General Motors* (New York: Henry Holt and Company, 1997), 55.

Socrates, "The shortest and surest..."
Thinkexist.com,http://www. thinkexist.com/English/Topic/x/Topic 2 30 3.htm.

Aristotle, "Dignity consists not..."
WorldofQuotes.com, http://www. worldofquotes.com/topic/Dignity/1/.

Pascal, "The heart has arguments..."
USBoomers.com, http://www. usboomerscom/quotes 2000.htm.

Thoreau, "Goodness is the only..."As quoted in Tom Morris, *If Aristotle Ran General Motors,* (New York: Henry Holt and Company, 1997), 115.

Concluding Thoughts on Ethical Excellence

" A society which is based on the letter of the law and never reaches higher is scarcely taking advantage of the high level of human possibilities."[1]
- Alexander Solzhenitsyn

Goodness is not often required in life. Like the other kinds of excellence, moral excellence is most often voluntary. To live a life of ethical excellence is to live by a standard of behavior that is beyond what is required by the law and, most often, beyond what is required by others.

Most people, unfortunately, tend to evaluate their own ethical behavior by comparing what they do with what others with whom they associate are doing. Studies suggest that in making such comparisons people tend to be easy on themselves, even perceiving themselves "to be far more ethical than comparable others."[2] Naturally, if we feel we are acting more ethically than most others around us, we are not going to feel that we need to improve.[3] We may, in fact, decide that the bad behavior of others is justification for our own indiscretions,[4] or even that otherwise unacceptable behavior, because it is widely engaged in, must be an acceptable part of life.[5]

It should be obvious that unless we see things as they really are, unless we are able to see ourselves in a truer light and determine that the appropriateness of our ethical behavior should be based on some standard other than what everyone else does, we will not make much progress as moral human beings. We will not be able to convince ourselves that people who act at a level of ethical excellence must act beyond what is required of them.

As Kant emphasizes in his third formulation, moral beings must respect the fact that all of us - self and others alike - are free to choose the course of our own self-perfection. High ethical standards cannot, by definition, be imposed upon us. At best, exceeding the legal standard can only be encouraged.

Throughout this book I have attempted to identify the discrete areas in which a person can demonstrate ethical excellence. However discrete the *Ethical Choice* may be, though, a careful examination will reveal that the choices are interrelated. Those who choose to be ethically excellent will not view the list of *Ethical Choices* as a menu from which they can choose "a little of this and a little of that." Excellence in being competent and diligent, for example, is part of our preparation to follow through with our ethical resolutions. People who are impartial spectators of their character and conduct will find that their ability to make well-reasoned decisions is enhanced.

As I conclude, let me reemphasize a few of the important ideas that can help the sincere person succeed in being ethically excellent:

- Ethical excellence is a choice that is unique and important, much like the choices we make regarding physical fitness, diet, workplace success, and marital and family success. With each of these choices, conventional behaviors will allow us to "get by" in life, but being excellent in all of these areas is worthy of our effort.

- The person who develops a disposition to be ethically excellent will most likely succeed in that effort. A disposition to do right results from making a commitment to do right all the time.

- Ethical excellence requires a level of exactness in doing what is right. Recognizing the details that need special attention, and then being willing to do what is required to make things right is the ethical person's quest. Significant attention needs to be given to those decisions where the common, but improper, practices of others tend to add justification for the action.

- Ethical excellence requires a level of sacrifice as we demonstrate a willingness to be other-centered. Sacrifices come in the form of time and personal advantage. Opportunities to sacrifice exist in fulfilling the day-to-day duties of our employment.

They also exist in the form of volunteerism. Sometimes recognizing the opportunities to serve others requires creative effort.

- Making complex decisions often requires significant effort. The ethically excellent person should be willing to set aside pride and personal preference and to consider the advice of others in arriving at the best decision. One of the important realities of dealing with moral issues in the workplace and in personal life is that the quick and most immediately painless fix is not always the best. The ethically excellent solution can require more effort and more sacrifice.

- Understanding how pressures, opportunities, and rationalizations affect actions can help in avoiding improper behaviors. Eliminating one or more of these three factors helps to ensure good behavior.

- The ability to be an impartial spectator of personal character and conduct is perhaps the most difficult challenge in succeeding in becoming ethically excellent. Bad habits, observing the low standards of others, and false perceptions of what it takes to succeed can reinforce behaviors that are not consistent with excellence.

A wise educator writing nearly a hundred years ago observed that the "supreme end of education is expert discernment in all things - the power to tell the good from the bad, the genuine from the counterfeit, and to prefer the good and the genuine to the bad and the counterfeit."[6] Today it is likely that a great many if not most people would respond that the goal of education is to get a better job.

I have spent my professional life observing what can happen when people care less about the good and more about "success." I have spent a goodly portion of the last several years thinking about what my observations have taught me. The request of a fine young son embarking upon a challenging career impelled me to bring my thoughts together in this book. And now I am ready to make a plea to all those, young and old, who want to live happy lives:

Work hard at being good. Strive for ethical excellence with as much diligence as you devote to getting ahead in your profession. Be as vigilant in maintaining your moral bearings as you are in keeping your health or your looks. Resolve that in all areas of your life you will do what is right, before you forget what that means. Examine yourself; determine where you need to improve. Resolve, prepare, and then follow through. I promise that you will be glad you did.

Notes

1   As quoted in A.L. Minkes "Business Policy, Ethics and Society" *Journal of Business Ethics,* 14 (1995): 596.

2   Thomas Tyson, "Does Believing that Everyone Else is Less Ethical have an Impact on Work Behavior?" *Journal of Business Ethics*, 11 (1992): 707.

3   O.C. Farrell and K. M. Weaver, "Ethical Beliefs of Marketing Managers," *Journal of Marketing*, July 1978: 69-73.

4   J.W. Newstrom and W.A. Ruch, "The Ethics of Management and the Management of Ethics," *MSU Business Topics*, Winter 1975: 36.

5   L.F. Pitt, and R. Abratt, "Corruption in Business: Are Management Attitudes Right?," *Journal of Business Ethics,* 5 (1986): 39.

6   As quoted in Tom Morris, *If Aristotle Ran General Motors* (New York: Henry Holt and Company, 1997), 210. This quotation is often misattributed to Samuel Johnson. It is actually a quotation from Charles Grosvenor Osgood's,1917 preface to Boswell's *Life of Johnson*. Osgood (1871-1964), Holmes Professor of Belles Lettres at Princeton, "was distinguished for the breadth of his learning and the influence of his teaching." http://etcweb1.princeton.edu/CampusWWW/Companion/osgood_charles.html.

Acknowledgments

I express my sincere thanks to many who have assisted in the preparation of this book. First, I thank my wife, Judy, for endorsing the effort and providing valuable insights in both the form and substance of the book. Next, I thank my children, David, Jared, Juliet, Heather, Jason, and Jennifer; my daughters-in-law Rebecca and Becca, and my son-in-law Toby Tilford, all of whom have assisted in many ways in this effort. I thank my extended family, including my parents, Verl and Mona Funk, my brother Ron, and my brother-in-law Cleon Butterfield and his wife Marci for their valuable examples and personal assistance in the editing process. Further, each of these and other family members has demonstrated characteristics of excellence in ethics that have affected my life in the most positive ways.

I thank the individuals at Promontory Publishing, namely Keith E. Garner, Susan Stewart, David L. Bird, and Michael A. Dunn who encouraged and inspired me to complete this effort and offered considerable assistance throughout the editing and publication process.

I thank the many people who likewise provided valuable assistance, especially Donlu Thayer, whose final editing contributed greatly to the finished product. I also express appreciation to Martin MacNeill, Kathleen Goodwin, Gary Nelson, Deborah McBride, Evan Byington, Gil A. Miller, Raani Erekson, and Jeffrey S. Pickett.

Finally, I gratefully acknowledge the many wise men and women of the ages whose ideas are incorporated into these pages, especially Adam Smith, Marcus Aurelius, Socrates, Plato, Aristotle, Immanuel Kant, and Victor Hugo. Additionally, a host of modern-day philosophers have been represented, including Tom Morris, Richard T. DeGeorge, Donelson R. Forsyth, Lawrence Kohlberg, Albert Bandura, Janet McCracken, William Martin, Bill Shaw, Larry C. Jensen, Steven A. Wygant, Surendra Arjoon, Ronald R. Sims, Oliver F. Williams, John W. Houch, Samuel V. Bruton, Milton Friedman, Louis Finkelstein, Peter F. Drucker, James Q. Wilson, Stephen L. Carter, and David Olive. It has been my diligent effort to represent their valuable ideas fairly and to acknowledge their contributions.

Bibliography

Altria. "Altria Code of Conduct for Compliance and Integrity."
http://www.altria.com.

American Institute of Certified Public Accountants. *AICPA Professional Standards: Code of Professional as of June 1, 1996.* Jersey City, New Jersey: Commerce Clearing House, 1996.

American International Group, Inc. "Code of Conduct." http//www.
AIGcorporate.com.

American Marketing Association. "Full Text of the AMA Code of Ethics."
http//www.3-media.com.

American Medical Association. "Principles of Medical Ethics, June 2001." http://
www.ama-assn.org.

Ames, William. *Conscience with the Power and Cases Thereof, n.p.* London: University Microfilms, Inc., 1639.

Arjoon, Surendra. "Virtue Theory as a Dynamic Theory of Business." *Journal of Business Ethics* 28 (2000): 159-178.

Argandona, Antonio. "The Stakeholder Theory and the Common Good." *Journal of Business Ethics* 17 (1998): 1093-1102.

AT&T. "2003 Code of Ethics." http://www.thecorporatelibrary.net.

Backof, Jeanne F. and Charles L. Martin, Jr. "Historical Perspectives: Development of the Codes of Ethics in Legal, Medical and Accounting Professions." *Journal of Business Ethics* 10 (1991): 99-110.

Bandura, Albert. *Social Foundations of Thought and Action,* Englewood Cliffs, New Jersey: Prentice-Hall, Inc., 1996.

Bassiry, G.R. and Marc Jones. "Adam Smith and the Ethics of Contemporary Capitalism." *Journal of Business Ethics* 12 (1993): 621-627.

Bennett, William J. *Our Sacred Honor.* Nashville, Tennessee: Broadman & Holman Publishers, 1997.

Berkshire Hathaway Inc. "Code of Business Conduct and Ethics." http://www.
precisionbrand.com.

Blundel, William E. "Some Assets Missing, Insurance Called Bogus at Equity Funding Life." *Wall Street Journal,* April, 2, 1973.

Boeing. "Code of Conduct." http://www.boeing.com.

Borowski, Paul J. "Manager – Employee Relationships: Guided by Kant's Categorical Imperative or by Dilbert's Business Principle." *Journal of Business Ethics* 17 (1998): 1623-1632.

Boulay, Art. "Malden Mills, A Study in Leadership." *Quality Monitor Newsletter*, October 1996.

Brainey Quote. http://www.brainyquote.com.

Bruton, Samuel V. "Teaching the Golden Rule." *Journal of Business Ethics* 49 (2004): 179-187.

Camenisch, Paul F. "Marketing Ethics: Some Dimensions of the Challenge." *Journal of Business Ethics* 10 (1991): 245-248.

Cameron, George D. III. "Ethics and Equity: Enforcing Ethical Standards in Commercial Relationships." *Journal of Business Ethics* 23 (2000): 161-172.

Carr, Albert Z. "Is Business Bluffing Ethical?" *Harvard Business Review* (Jan-Feb 1968):143-153.

Carson, Thomas L. "Conflicts of Interest." *Journal of Business Ethics* 13 (1994): 387-404.

Carter, Stephen L. *Civility.* New York: HarperPerennial, 1998.

Carter, Stephen L. *Integrity.* New York: BasicBooks, 1996.

CBS News. "The Mensch of Malden Mills." July 6, 2003. http://www.CBSNews.com.

ChevronTexaco. "Business Conduct & Ethics." http://www.chevrontexaco.com.

Chismar, Douglas. "Vice and Virtue in Everyday (Business) Life." *Journal of Business Ethics* 29 (2001): 169-176.

Citigroup. "Code of Conduct." http://www.citigroup.com.

Classical Library. http://www.classicallibrary.org.

Cleary, Thomas, trans. *Living the Good Life, Advice on Virtue, Love and Action from the Ancient Greek Masters.* Boston & London: Shambhala, 1997.

Coker, Edward W. "Adam Smith's Concept of the Social System." *Journal of Business Ethics* 9 (1990): 139-142.

Columbia World of Quotations. Http://www.bartleby.com.

Cooke, Robert Allan. "Danger Signs of Unethical Behavior: How to Determine If Your Firm Is at Ethical Risk." *Journal of Business Ethics* 10 (1991): 249-253.

Coolidge, Shelley Donald. "'Corporate Decency' Prevails at Malden Mills." *Christian Science Monitor*, Mar 28, 1996, 1-9.

Cosier, R.A. and C.R. Schwenk. "Agreement and Thinking Alike: Ingredients for Poor Decisions." *Academy of Management Executive* 4 (February 1990): 69-75.

Covey, Stephen R. *Principle-Centered Leadership*. New York: Simon & Schuster, 1990.

Covey, Stephen R. *Seven Habits of Highly Successful People*. New York: Simon & Schuster, 1989.

Creative Quotations. Http://www.creativequotations.com

Cunningham, W. Patrick. "The Golden Rule as Universal Ethical Norm." *Journal of Business Ethics* 17 (1998): 105-109.

Dante. Henry W. Longfellow, trans. *The Divine Comedy*.

Dawson, David. "Virtues, Managers and Business People: Finding a Place for MacIntyre in a Business Context." *Journal of Business Ethics* 48 (2003): 127-138.

Deckop, John R., Carol C. Cirka and Lynne M. Andersson. "Doing Unto Others: The Reciprocity of Helping Behavior in Organizations." *Journal of Business Ethics* 47 (2003): 101-113.

De George, Richard T. *Business Ethics, Fourth Edition*. New Jersey: Prentice Hall, 1995.

Drucker, Peter F. "The Unfashionable Kierkegaard." *The New Markets and Other Essays* (1971).

Dunkelberg, John and Debra Ragin Jessup. "So Then Why Did You Do It?" *Journal of Business Ethics* 29 (2001): 51-63.

Enneagram. Http.//www.enneagramtest.com.

Evin, Robert E. "Corporate Loyalty: Its Objects and Its Grounds." *Journal of Business Ethics* 12 (1993): 387-396.

Executive Forum. http://www.executive-forum.com.

ExxonMobil. "Standards of Business Conduct." http://www.ExxonMobil.com.

FannieMae. "Code of Ethics." http://www.fanniemae.com.

Farrell, O.C. and K.M. Weaver. "Ethical Beliefs of Marketing Managers." *Journal of Marketing* (July 1978): 69-73.

Finkelstein, Louis. "The Businessman's Moral Failure." *Fortune Magazine*, September 1958.

Ford Motor Company. "2003 Code of Ethics." http://www.thecorporatelibrary.net.

Forsyth, Donelson R. "Judging the Morality of Business Practices: The Influence of Personal Moral Philosophies." *Journal of Business Ethics* 11 (1992): 461-470.

Franklin, Benjamin. *Autobiography* from *The Works of Benjamin Franklin*. New York: G.P. Putman's Sons, 1904.

Frey, Donald E. "Individualist Economic Values and Self-Interest: The Problem in the Puritan Ethic." *Journal of Business Ethics* 17 (1998): 1573-1580.

Friedman, Milton. "The Social Responsibility of Business is to Increase Profits." *New York Times Magazine,* September 13, 1970.

Fusfeld, Daniel R. "Adam Smith." *World Book Encyclopedia* 17 (1981): 425.

General Electric. "General Electric: Our Commitment: Integrity." http://www.ge.com.

Giacalone, Robert A. and Stephen B. Knouse. "Justifying Wrongful Employee Behavior: The Role of Personality in Organizational Sabotage." *Journal of Business Ethics* 9 (1990): 55-61.

Goodman, Ted, ed. *The Forbes Book of Business Quotations*. New York: Black Dog & Leventhal Publishers, 1997.

Greenspan, Alan. "Remarks by Chairman Alan Greenspan, Commencement Address, Harvard University." (June 10, 1999).

Gross-Schaefer, Arthur, Jeff Trigilio, Jamie Negus, and Ceng-Si Ro. "Ethics Education in the Workplace: An Effective Tool to Combat Employee Theft." *Journal of Business Ethics* 26 (2000): 89-100.

Haksever, Cengiz, Radha Chaganti, and Ronald G. Cook. "A Model of Value Creation: Strategic View." *Journal of Business Ethics* 49 (2004): 291-305.

Heckman, Peter. "Business and Games." *Journal of Business Ethics* 11 (1992): 933-938.

Hill, John. "Can We Talk About Ethics Anymore?" *Journal of Business Ethics* 14 (1995): 585-592.

Holley, David M. "Information Disclosure in Sales." *Journal of Business Ethics* 17 (1998): 631-641.

Home Depot. "Business Code of Conduct and Ethics." http://www.homedepot.com.

Hugo, Victor. Norman Denny, trans. *Les Miserables*. London, England: Penguin Books, 1976.

Hunt, Eugene H. and Ronald K. Bullis. "Applying the Principles of Gestalt Theory to Teaching Ethics." *Journal of Business Ethics* 10 (1991): 341-347.

Ibrahim, Nabil A., Leslie W. Rue, Patricia P. McDougall, and G. Robert Greene. "Characteristics and Practice of 'Christian-Based' Companies." *Journal of Business Ethics* 10 (1991): 123-132.

Jayaraman, L.L. and Byung K. Min. "Business Ethics—A Developmental Perspective: The Evolution of the Free and Mature Corporation." *Journal of Business Ethics* 12 (1993): 665-675.

Jensen, Larry C and Steven A. Wygant. "The Developmental Self-Valuing Theory: A Practical Approach for Business Ethics." *Journal of Business Ethics* 9 (1990): 215-225.

Jurkiewicz, Carole L. and Robert A. Giacalone. "A Values Framework for Measuring the Impact of Workplace Spirituality on Organizational Performance." *Journal of Business Ethics* 49 (2004): 129-142.

Kahneman, Daniel, Jack L. Knetsch and Richard Thaler. "Fairness as a Constraint on Profit Seeking: Entitlements in the Market." *American Economic Review* 76 (September 1986): 728-741.

Kalwall. "Malden Mills, Daylight From Ashes." http://www.kalwall.com.

Kant, Immanuel. *Foundations of the Metaphysics of Morals,* 1785. New York: MacMillian, 1990.

Kelley, Patricia C. and Dawn R. Elm. "The Effect of Context on Moral Intensity of Ethical Issues: Revising Jones's Issue – Contingent Model." *Journal of Business Ethics* 48 (2003): 139-154.

Kjonstad, Bjorn and Hugh Willmott. "Business Ethics: Restrictive or Empowering." *Journal of Business Ethics* 14 (1995): 445-464.

Koehn, Daryl. "Can and Should Businesses Be Friends with One Another and with Their Stakeholders." *Journal of Business Ethics* 17 (1998): 1755-1763.

Koehn, Daryl. "Ethical Issues Connected with Multi-Level Marketing Schemes." *Journal of Business Ethics* 29 (2001): 153-160.

Kohlberg, Lawrence. "The Claim to Moral Adequacy of a Highest Stage of Moral Judgment." *The Journal of Philosophy* (1973): 630-646.

Korsgard, Christine. *Creating the Kingdom of Ends.* New York: Cambridge University Press, 1996.

The Kroger Co. "The Kroger Co. Policy on Business Ethics." http://www.kroger.com.

Laczniak, Gene R. and Patrick E. Murphy. "Fostering Ethical Marketing Decisions." *Journal of Business Ethics* 10 (1991): 259-271.

Ladd, John. "Morality and the Ideal of Rationality in Formal Organizations." *The Monist, An International Quarterly Journal of General Philosophical Inquiry* 54 (Oct 1970): 488-516.

Lee, Rex E. "Honesty and Integrity." *BYU Speeches* (September 5, 1995).

Lere, John C. and Bruce R. Gaumnitz. "The Impact of Codes of Ethics on Decision Making: Some Insights from Information Economics." *Journal of Business Ethics* 48 (2003): 365-379.

Liberty-Tree. http://www.quotes.liberty-tree.ca.

Long, George, trans. *The Meditations of Marcus Aurelius.* New York: Avon Books, 1993.

Lowry, Diannah. "An Investigation of Student Moral Awareness and Associated Factors in Two Cohorts of an Undergraduate Business Degree in a British University: Implications for Business Ethics Curriculum Design." *Journal of Business Ethics* 48 (2003):7-19.

Lurie, Yotam. "Humanizing Business through Emotions: On the Role of Emotions in Ethics." *Journal of Business Ethics* 49 (2004): 1-11.

Maclagan, Patrick. "Varieties of Moral Issue and Dilemma: A Framework for the Analysis of Case Material in Business Ethics Education." *Journal of Business Ethics* 48 (2003): 21-32.

Manchester, William. *The Last Lion, Winston Spencer Churchill, Visions of Glory.* Boston and Toronto: Little, Brown and Company, 1983.

Marana, G.P. *Letters Writ by a Turkish Spy.* Vol iv, Book III, letter 10.

McCracken, Janet, William Martin and Bill Shaw. "Virtue Ethics and the Parable of the Sadhu." *Journal of Business Ethics* 17 (1998): 25-38.

McCullough, David. *Truman.* New York: Simon & Schuster, 1992.

McKesson Corporation. "Code of Business Conduct and Ethics." http:/www.mckesson.com.

McLain, David L. and John P. Keenan. "Risk, Information, and the Decision about Response to Wrongdoing in an Organization." *Journal of Business Ethics* 19 (1999): 255-271.

Mellema, Gregory. "Business Ethics and Doing What One Ought to Do." *Journal of Business Ethics* 13 (1994): 149-153.

Memorable Quotations. http://www.memorablequotations.com.

Microsoft Corporation. "Delivering on Our Mission." http://www.microsoft.com.

Minkes, A.L. "Business Policy, Ethics and Society." *Journal of Business Ethics* 14 (1995): 593-601.

Molyneaux, David. "'Blessed Are the Meek, for They Shall Inherit the Earth' – An Aspiration Applicable to Business?" *Journal of Business Ethics* 48 (2003): 347-363.

Morris, Tom. *If Aristotle Ran General Motors*. New York: Henry Holt and Company, 1997.

Motivating Quotes. Http://www.motivatingquotes.com.

Narveson, Jan. "The 'Invisible Hand.'" *Journal of Business Ethics* 46 (2003): 201-212.

National Education Association. "Code of Ethics of the Education Profession." http://www.nea.org.

National Society of Professional Engineers. "NSPE Code of Ethics for Engineers." http://www.nspe.org.

Nelson, Julianne. "Business Ethics in a Competitive Market." *Journal of Business Ethics* 13 (1994): 663-666.

Newbert, Scott L. "Realizing the Spirit and Impact of Adam Smith's Capitalism through Entrepreneurship." *Journal of Business Ethics* 46 (2003): 251-261.

Newstrom J.W. and W.A. Ruch. "The Ethics of Management and the Management of Ethics." *MSU Business Topics* (Winter 1975): 36.

O'Boyle, Edward J. and Lyndon E. Dawson, Jr. "The American Marketing Association Code of Ethics: Instructions for Marketers." *Journal of Business Ethics* 11 (1992): 921-932.

Olive, David. *Just Rewards: The Case for Ethical Reform in Business*. Toronto: Key Porter Books, 1987.

O'Neil, Robert F. and Darlene A. Pienta. "Economic Criteria Versus Ethical Criteria Toward Resolving a Basic Dilemma in Business." *Journal of Business Ethics* 13 (1994): 71-78.

Otten, A.L. "Ethics on the Job: Companies Alert Employees to Potential Dilemmas." *The Wall Street Journal*, July 14, 1986, 17.

Pava, Moses L. "The Substance of Jewish Business Ethics." *Journal of Business Ethics* 17 (1998): 603-617.

Pava, Moses L. "Religious Business Ethics and Political Liberalism: An Integrative Approach." *Journal of Business Ethics* 17 (1998): 1633-1652.

Pava, Moses L., Jeremy Pava, and Joel Hochman. "Fairness as a Constraint in the Real Estate Market." *Journal of Business Ethics* 19 (1999): 91-97.

Pava, Moses L. "Searching for Spirituality in All the Wrong Places." *Journal of Business Ethics* 48 (2003): 393-400.

Pearson, Gordon and Martin Parker. "The Relevance of Ancient Greeks to Modern Business? A Dialogue on Business and Ethics." *Journal of Business Ethics* 31 (2001): 341-353.

Pennar, K., P. Galuska, D. Lindoff, and R. Jesurum. "The Destructive Costs of Greasing Palms." *Business Week*, December 6, 1993.

Phillips, Donald T. *Lincoln on Leadership*. New York: Warner Books, 1992.

PI Profiles International. http://www.AssessmentCompany.com.

Pitt, L.F. and R. Abratt. "Corruption in Business: Are Management Attitudes Right?" *Journal of Business Ethics* 5 (1986): 39.

Primeaux, Patrick and John Stieber. "Profit Maximization: The Ethical Mandate of Business." *Journal of Business Ethics* 13 (1994): 287-294.

Quote Lady. Http://www.quotelady.com.

Quote World. Http://www.quoteworld.org.

Rivoli, Pietra. "Ethical Aspects of Investor Behavior." *Journal of Business Ethics* 14 (1995): 265-277.

Rossouw, Gedeon Josua. "Business Ethics: Where Have All the Christians Gone?" *Journal of Business Ethics* 13 (1994): 557-570.

Schermerhorn, J.R. *Management for Productivity*, New York: John Wiley, 1989.

Schwartz, Michael. "Peter Drucker and the Denial of Business Ethics." *Journal of Business Ethics* 17 (1998): 1685-1692.

Sethi, S. Parakash and Paul Steidlmeier. "Religion's Moral Compass and a Just Economic Order: Reflections on Pope John Paul II's Encyclical *Centesimus Annus.*" *Journal of Business Ethics* 12 (1993): 901-917.

Shakespeare, William. *Henry V.*

Shaw, Bill and Frederick R. Post. "A Moral Basis for Corporate Philanthropy." *Journal of Business Ethics* 12 (1993): 745-751.

Shaw, William H. and Vincent Barry. *Moral Issues in Business*. Belmont, California: Wadsworth, 1999.

Silverstein, S. "One in 15 Employees in Study Caught Stealing." *Los Angeles Times*, December 2, 1989, D-1.

Sims, Ronald R. "The Challenge of Ethical Behavior in Organizations." *Journal of Business Ethics* 11 (1992): 505-513.

Sims, Ronald R. "Linking Groupthink to Unethical Behavior in Organizations." *Journal of Business Ethics* 11 (1992): 651-662.

Smeltzer, Larry R. and Marianne M. Jennings. "Why An International Code of Business Ethics Would Be Good for Business." *Journal of Business Ethics* 17 (1998): 57-66.

Smith, Adam. D.D. Raphael and A.L. Aacfie, eds. *The Theory of Moral Sentiments.* Indianapolis, Liberty Fund, 1984.

Smith, Adam. *An Inquiry into the Nature and Causes of the Wealth of Nations.* New York: The Modern Library, 1965.

Smith, Wallace F. "Readers Report." *Business Week,* May 4, 1992.

Snider, Jamie, Ronald Paul Hill and Diane Martin. "Corporate Social Responsibility in the 21st Century: A View from the World's Most Successful Firms." *Journal of Business Ethics* 48 (2003): 175-187.

Society for Human Resource Management. "Code of Ethics." http://www.hutchshrm.org.

Sullivan, Roger J. "A Response to 'Is Business Bluffing Ethical?'" *Business and Professional Ethics Journal,* 1-18.

Teal, Thomas. "Not a Fool, Not a Saint." *Fortune Magazine,* November 11, 1996, 201-204.

Thought-of-the-Day Archive. http://www.refdesk.com.

Tyson, Thomas. "Does Believing that Everyone Else is Less Ethical have an Impact on Work Behavior?" *Journal of Business Ethics* 11 (1992): 707-717.

Ulrich, Peter and Ulrich Thielemann. "How Do Managers Think about Market Economies and Morality? Empirical Enquiries into Business-ethical Thinking Patterns." *Journal of Business Ethics* 12 (1993): 879-898.

UPS. "UPS Code of Business Conduct." http://www.ups.com.

Van Buren, Harry J. III. "Acting More Generously than the Law Requires: The Issue of Employee Layoffs in *halakhah*." *Journal of Business Ethics* 19 (1999): 335-343.

Van Es, Robert. "Inside and Outside *The Insider*: A Film Workshop in Practical Ethics." *Journal of Business Ethics* 48 (2003): 89-97.

Vredenburgh, Donald and Yael Brender. "The Hierarchical Abuse of Power in Work Organizations." *Journal of Business Ethics* 17 (1998): 1337-1347.

WalMart. "Statement of Ethics." http://www.walmartstores.com.

Watson, Charles E. "Managing With Integrity: Social Responsibilities of Business as Seen by America's CEOs." *Business Horizons,* Jul-Aug 1991: 99-109.

Weber, James and Sharon Green. "Principled Moral Reasoning: Is it a Viable Approach to Promote Ethical Integrity?" *Journal of Business Ethics* 10 (1991): 325-333.

Williams, Oliver F. and John W. Houch, eds. *A Virtuous Life in Business.* Lanham, Maryland: Rowman & Littlefield Publishers, Inc., 1992.

Williams, Oliver F. and John W. Houch, eds. *The Judeo-Christian Vision and the Modern Corporation.* University of Notre Dame Press, 1982.
> Bennett, John C. "3. Protestantism and Corporations." 83-105.
> Schall, James V. "4. Catholicism, Business, and Human Priorities." 107-140.
> Seiser, Burton M. "5. The Rabbinic Tradition and Corporate Morality." 141-155.

Wilson, James Q. *The Moral Sense.* New York: The Free Press, 1993.

Wood, David. "Business Justice: Transactions, Resources, and Organisations." *Journal of Business Ethics* 13 (1994): 481-486.

World of Quotes. Http://www.worldofquotes.com.

World's Greatest Sports Quotes. http://www.inspirational-quotes.org.

Young, A. Thomas. "Ethics in Business." *Vital Speeches of the Day* (September 15, 1992): 725-726.

Index